Women in Canadian

Literature

M.G. McClung

**Preface by
George Woodcock**

Women in Canadian Life

**General Editors:
Jean Cochrane
Pat Kincaid**

Fitzhenry & Whiteside

Women in Canadian Life Series
Women in Canadian Literature

General Editors:
Jean Cochrane
Journalist,
Educational Media Consultant

Pat Kincaid
Women's Studies Consultant,
Toronto Board of Education

About the Author
Molly McClung, an English specialist, has taught at both secondary and university levels in Kingston, Ontario, and has acted as a resource person for a variety of groups developing materials for courses involving women in literature. When not teaching or writing, she is likely to be engaged in soapstone sculpture.

This series begins with books centering on the themes of politics, sports, literature and the law. Other themes to be discussed in this series include communications, science and technology, education, medicine, art and the labour force.

Design:
F. W. Hindle, Béatrice Dermaut

Cover Illustration:
Terry Shoffner

Printed and bound in Canada

ISBN 0-88902-378-6

Illustration Credits

Special thanks to Kate Hamilton, the League of Canadian Poets, Arnaud Maggs, and John Reeves.
British Columbia Archives 30B
Canadian Broadcasting Corporation 28
Fitzhenry & Whiteside Collection 29
General/Musson Publishing 49
Imperial Oil Review 59, 60
Jewish Historical Society of Western Canada, Inc. 58T
League of Canadian Poets 36M, 36B, 37T, 39T, 40T, 41T
Dr. Stuart Macdonald 21, 22
Manitoba Archives 33, 39B, 73B
McClelland & Stewart 51, 57
Metropolitan Toronto Library Board 13, 31B, 36T, 55T, 73T, 90
Miller Services 61T
Mirror Newspapers 66
Public Archives of Canada 6 (C-524), 8 (C-11227), 9 (PA-45005), 10 (C-9510), 11 (C-9368, C-9482), 12 (C-7043), 13B (C-18164), 16 (C-6720), 17 (C-6197), 18 (C-46354), 20 (C-6724), 23 (C-89584), 24 (C-7780), 27 (C-5482), 31T (C-36086), 32 (C-30953), 37B (C-47066), 46 (C-18347), 47 (PA-43753), 50 (C-2016), 52 (PA-22619)
John Reeves 43
Toronto Star/Ron Bull 41B
University of Toronto 74, 76, 79, 83, 84, 86, 87
University of Toronto Libraries 19, 38, 40B, 55B, 64, 65, 67
Vancouver Art Gallery 30T
Writers' Union of Canada 61B, 68
Writers' Union/Arnaud Maggs 58B

Every effort has been made to credit all illustration sources correctly. The publishers welcome further information in order to rectify possible inaccuracies in future editions.

Contents

Preface

The first novel concerning Canada, *The History of Emily Montague* (1769), was written more than two hundred years ago by a woman, Frances Brooke, who knew the famous Dr. Samuel Johnson. Frances Brooke was a transient member of the British garrison society in Quebec after the conquest, but other women came whose commitment to Canada was lifelong, and it is hard to think what writing in this country would have been like in those vital decades after the War of 1812 if it had not been for Susanna Moodie and Catherine Parr Traill and Anna Jameson, with their extraordinary sketches of the early settlements of Upper Canada, which combined the observation of a young and developing society with the intense personal dramas of adjustment that attended the transplanting of English gentlewomen to the backwoods and clearings of early Canada.

In the pages that follow, the stories of such women are part of the tapestry of our culture which *Women in Canadian Literature* creates. What is important in having a survey of this kind is that for the first time one becomes really aware of the vital and growing contribution the women of our society have made to Canadian writing.

The contribution, as I have suggested, is dramatically there at the beginning in the fact that what we know in literary terms of the life of Upper Canadian settlers is seen mostly through the eyes of women. During the later decades, as the North American colonies settle into Confederation, women writers become temporarily less prominent. In the last half of the nineteenth century, however, there is at least one leading Canadian poet who was a woman, Isabella Valancy Crawford, and one very remarkable social novelist, Sara Jeannette Duncan, whom I believe to have been the best Canadian fiction writer of her time.

A remarkable feature of women's writing in Canada during the nineteenth century — for which I have never found a satisfactory explanation — is the absence of good poets. There were dozens of charming versifiers, and some of them — like Pauline Johnson — were very theatrical in their public readings. But Isabella Crawford is the only woman poet of any real stature before Dorothy Livesay began to write during the late 1920s. In Quebec the process of late development applied in both prose and poetry; there was no major woman novelist writing in Canada in French before the appearance of Gabrielle Roy, and no considerable woman poet before Anne Hébert.

The changes since those days have been immense and exhilarating. Today women writers not merely compete on an equal level with men; there are many years when they dominate the publishers' lists, and today, in the late 1970s, we can look back on the careers of many women writers who have become classics in their own lifetime. Dorothy Livesay, of course, is one of them. Another is Margaret Laurence, who has produced during the past twenty years a series of novels and collections of stories which — even if she keeps to her threat of writing no fiction after *The Diviners* — assures her a permanent place among the handful of major Canadian novelists. If I write with a little less certainty about Margaret Atwood, it is not from any doubt of her remarkable talents but because of my unsureness as to where to place her, since she is one of our best poets, a remarkable and original novelist, and also a very astute and imaginative critic; perhaps one should class her as Canada's first true woman of letters.

Women in Canadian Literature is an excellent introduction to the past record of women in Canadian writing, and to the extraordinary present, in which it is hard to imagine our literary world without people like Laurence and Atwood, like Dorothy Livesay and Gwen MacEwen and Marian Engel, like Audrey Thomas and Jay Macpherson and Alice Munro, like P. K. Page and Sheila Watson and Phyllis Webb, like — and here is a name that must be spoken alone, in esteem and gratitude — Ethel Wilson. For if any single writer liberated Canadian fiction from the national self-consciousness that gathered over it in Hugh MacLennan's 1940s and 1950s, it was this marvellously urbane woman, who began writing late in life, wrote for only a few years and produced a scanty handful of slim novels and one book of stories, yet by her lyrical ironies brought Canadian fiction back to recognition that the proper study of humankind is man and woman in the infinite variety of their relationships and solitudes.

The literary upsurge in Canada during the past twenty years has thus been in any terms amazing, but perhaps most amazing in the high proportion of the new and vital writers who have been women. And it is the women who have given the characteristic flavour to Canadian writing in the 1960s and 1970s. As editor of *Canadian Literature* I have had the pleasure of publishing work by a great number of writers whose names appear in *Women in Canadian Literature,* and as a writer I can count many of them among my cherished friends; I am glad to see their talents celebrated in this timely account of what women have contributed to that veritable renaissance of a nation's literature through which we have been living since the 1950s.

George Woodcock
Vancouver, July 1977

Chapter 1

Beginnings

Canada's first visitors were explorers, closely followed by those who came to exploit its riches in furs and timber. The first settlers, in the Maritimes and Quebec, came from Europe to take up free land. To protect them and the various colonial boundaries came the military garrisons. A European population grew slowly on the East Coast and St. Lawrence shores, pushing the native population westward. Those actually farming were involved in back-breaking labour and had no leisure time; those in senior civil and military positions could find the time to write if they chose to do so. For these reasons, the first Canadian literature sent back to England and France consisted mainly of upper-class accounts of the "new land" — letters, diaries, descriptions of voyages: attempts to pin down on paper the vastness of the forested land and its climatic extremes.

The first women writers were the educated ladies whose lives in England, before visiting or emigrating to Canada, had given them a high sense of the value of arts and letters. They often had previous experience in writing. The first to be associated with Canada, in spite of popular trends at the time, was not a diarist but a novelist.

Frances Brooke (1724-1789) was an English poet, essayist and playwright. In 1763, before her Canadian venture, her first novel appeared anonymously. *The History of Lady Julia Mandeville* contains some Canadian material, presumably taken from letters and reports. She then joined her husband, the Rev. John

Brooke, who was chaplain to the British garrison at Quebec from 1760 to 1768. On their return to England, she wrote *The History of Emily Montague* (1769), based on her own observations of Quebec City. This time her name appeared on the title-page.

In Frances Brooke's time the novel was a new literary form, only in its second generation. In her novels, Frances Brooke followed the fiction conventions that prevailed in London: the epistolary and sentimental modes. *The History of Emily Montague,* in over two hundred letters, charts the romantic problems of six well-bred young people of the "age of sensibility." The general background is the social life among the privileged classes in Quebec City and England. Today this novel is usually read for its pictures of the young colony and the surrounding countryside. The attitude to the physical character of Canada is perhaps inevitable, and sets the tone for the next century of writing.

> On approaching the coast of America, I felt a kind of religious veneration, on seeing rocks which almost touch'd the clouds, cover'd with tall groves of pines that seemed coeval with the world itself: to which veneration the solemn silence not a little contributed . . .

Frances Brooke includes a wealth of comment (from an upper-class and British bias) on the local societies, English, French and Indian.

An immigrant's first view of Canada: the mouth of the St. Lawrence River

Elizabeth Simcoe

This somewhat Canadian novel came to the attention of Elizabeth Simcoe, a wealthy young English society woman. Her husband, Colonel John Graves Simcoe, was appointed Lieutenant-Governor of Upper Canada in 1791, when what was known as "Canada" was divided into Upper and Lower provinces. With six children under the age of eight, she was suddenly called to go to what was close to wilderness. Leaving the four eldest cared for in England, she travelled to Quebec City and on to the smaller city of Montreal (mainly a fur centre at that time), then to Newark (Niagara), the temporary capital.

The rigours of bad housing, winter, and constant servant problems did little to daunt her spirit, nor did a winter of living in tents while new quarters were under construction in York (now Toronto). Of course, her standing as "first lady of the land" helped.

Elizabeth Simcoe's *Diary* (first published over a century later, in 1911) covers her five years in Newark and York. She was constantly travelling — by horse, canoe, carriage, sleigh, or on foot. In her diary, she described not people and events, though they are included, but the land itself: the plants, the fish, the boats. Everything was picturesque to her. She also used her training in drawing to sketch various scenes and to draw her husband's maps.

Life in Canada, as described by Frances Brooke and Elizabeth Simcoe, was the upper-class life as seen by women who were basically visitors. They knew they would eventually be returning to England, where children could be educated properly, where there was civilized and cultured company, and where the landscape was tamed and the weather moderate. In many ways they were spared the harsh realities of living in a new land.

The next phase of Canada's literary history is the documentation of the settler's rather than the visitor's life. British settlement in Nova Scotia increased after the fall of Louisburg in 1758. United Empire Loyalists displaced by the American Revolution came north to New Brunswick. Another six thousand Loyalists settled in Quebec's Eastern Townships and along the north shores of the upper St. Lawrence and Lake Ontario. After the Napoleonic Wars were over in 1815, a great wave of immigration from the United Kingdom began. There were crop failures in Ireland, and Scottish crofters were thrown off the land. The British military strength was reduced and many officers found that they could not subsist on half-pay. Free land across the Atlantic ocean sounded very attractive.

In 1825, Samuel Strickland, a young Englishman from a family of good education and little money, emigrated to Canada. His letters back home described his pioneering venture near Peterborough, Ontario, in positive terms. His sisters, Catherine and Susanna among them, were at the time contributing to the family finances by writing all kinds of popular literature — verse, fiction, and non-fiction, for both children and adults.

The Strickland homestead in Lakefield. Catherine Traill is third from the left, holding the baby; Samuel Strickland is second from the right.

In 1831 Susanna Strickland married John Moodie, a soldier and traveller, and her sister Catherine married his widower friend Thomas Traill in 1832. On the strength of Samuel Strickland's advice the Traills came to Canada in the same year. For a while Susanna Moodie fought her husband's desire to emigrate. However neither Susanna nor John had brought money or property to their love match, and their financial situation forced her to agree. They arrived in Quebec City only three weeks after the Traills, to be greeted by a cholera epidemic.

Catherine Parr (Strickland) Traill was the first of the sisters to record her journey and her early experiences, in *The Backwoods of Canada* (1836). She had a naturalist's turn of mind, a genuine love of nature, and an unsnobbish curiosity about her neighbours, nearby Indian villagers included. She wrote mainly for future British emigrant wives so that they would not suffer too much from culture shock. Her attitudes as well as her observations were useful:

> . . . it is considered by no means derogatory to the wife of an officer or gentleman to assist in the work of the house, or to perform its entire duties, if occasion requires it; to understand the mystery of soap, candle, and sugar-making; to make bread, butter, and cheese, or even to milk her own cows . . .

As it turned out, only Samuel Strickland really throve on pioneering. There were several moves during the next years in Catherine's life from the bush to more settled land.

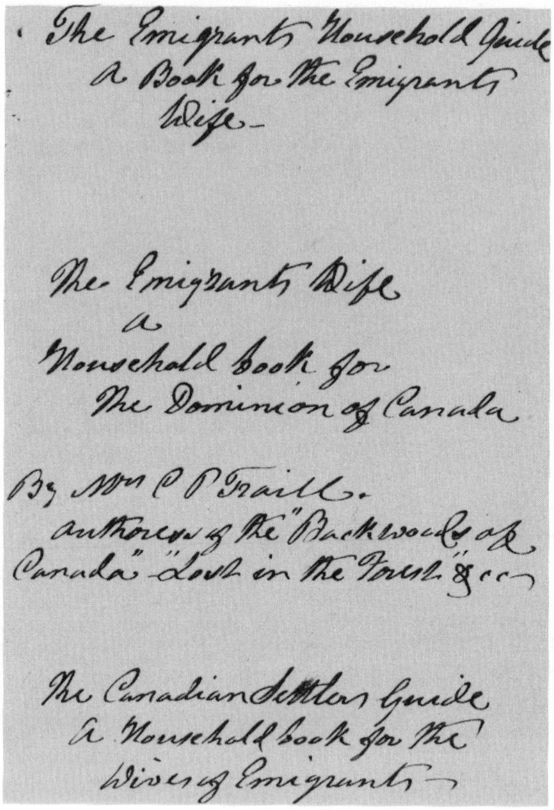

The Emigrants Household Guide
A Book for the Emigrants
Wife —

The Emigrants Wife
a
Household book for
The Dominion of Canada

By Mrs C P Traill.
authoress of the "Backwoods of
Canada" "Lost in the Forest" &c c

The Canadian Settlers Guide
a Household book for the
Wives of Emigrants

Traill's notes on titles for a new book. She chose The Canadian Settler's Guide.

In these slightly more civilized surroundings she went back to writing sentimental and romantic tales, and a collection of animal stories. In 1854, she put together *The Canadian Settler's Guide,* an immensely practical compendium on gardening, plants, foods and cooking, right down to the curing of meat and the preparation of dandelion roots as a coffee substitute. It can still serve as a guide for anyone who wants to go back to the land. Her botanical streak can also be seen in her *Canadian Wild Flowers* (1868) , and *Studies of Plant Life in Canada* (1884) , written in collaboration with her niece, Agnes FitzGibbon.

Her sister Susanna (Strickland) Moodie did not have the same cheerful outlook on emigration and farming. Her husband was ever the gentleman, not inclined to do the heavy manual labour of the true pioneer. At first he tried share-cropping on cleared land near Cobourg, where they spent their first winter in a shanty. The conditions were rough, and the neighbours (Irish, United Empire Loyalist, or whatever, they were usually "Yankees" to the very English Susanna) seemed very alien.

After this disastrous experience, the Moodies set off early in 1834 for the Peterborough district to be near Samuel and the

Traills. Here they were pioneers indeed, and the life was hard. Susanna's life of farming and raising children was made harder by the absence of John, off to fight the 1837 Rebellion, or to find any other gentlemanly occupation. Help came from an unexpected source. In 1837, John Lovell of Montreal was starting up a periodical, the *Literary Garland*. He wrote to Susanna, asking her for contributions and (most important) offering to pay for them. She reacted with enthusiasm.

> Strange as it may appear to the reader, these literary labours were a great refreshment to me, instead of an additional fatigue. They helped fill up the hungry void at my heart, occasioned by the long absence of my husband; and I forgot the hardships and privations of my lot, whilst rousing into action, after long disuse, the powers and energies of my mind.

As a result, a number of her sketches of "rough" pioneer life were to appear first in the *Literary Garland*.

The Moodies left the bush as soon as they could and moved to Belleville in 1839, where John worked himself into and out of various minor official positions. Susanna continued to write for a Canadian audience, but the small colony was not ready to support a lot of literature. The Moodies' joint venture into a periodical of their own, Belleville's *Victoria Magazine*, lasted through only twelve issues (1847-1848). The *Literary Garland* folded in 1851. The real market for writing was across the Atlantic ocean.

A letter from Susanna Moodie to Catherine Traill. To save paper, people would write first horizontally and then vertically, cutting paper use in half.

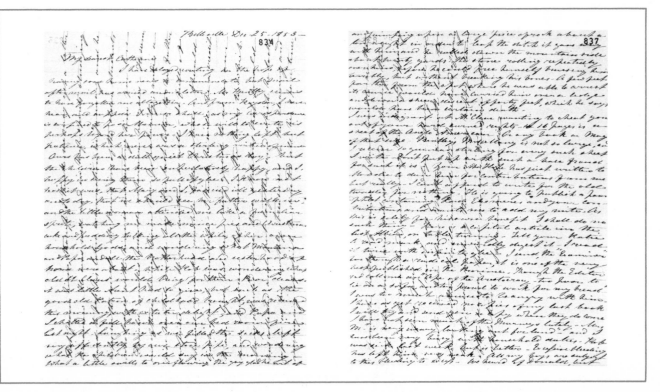

Susanna Moodie

I am afraid women deteriorate in this country more than the other sex. As long as the lady is necessarily the most active member of her household she keeps her ground from her utility; but when the state of semi-civilization arrives, and the delicacies of her table, and the elegancies of her person become her chief concern and pride, then she must fall, and must be contented to be looked upon as belonging merely to the decorative department of the establishment and valued accordingly.

from The Journals of Anne Langton *(Clarke, Irwin, 1950)*

Susanna collected her sketches and stories into *Rouging It in the Bush* (1852). Though some of them had been written for a Montreal audience, a good many had been written in Belleville and were directed to an English readership. Her ambivalent attitude toward the wilderness and her image of herself as an English lady set the tone of the book. The most famous passage, so much stronger than her sister's warnings about emigration, occurs at the very end:

> If these sketches should prove the means of deterring one family from sinking their property, and shipwrecking all their hopes, by going to reside in the backwoods of Canada, I shall consider myself amply repaid for revealing the secrets of the prison-house, and feel that I have not toiled and suffered in the wilderness in vain.

That, emphatically, spelled out Susanna Moodie's thoughts on "the bush," and Canadian reaction to this comment was severe.

Partly to counter the criticism, Susanna Moodie rapidly put together her *Life in the Clearings* (1853). In the introduction, she wrote much more favourably about Canada and was gracious even to Americans. As a book it seems much less personal than *Roughing It in the Bush. Life in the Clearings* is still valuable for its observations of Ontario in the middle of the nineteenth century, with its descriptions of camp meetings, the lunatic asylum, unusual characters, and the Provincial Agricultural Show.

For Susanna, that was the end of realistic writing, of sketching from direct observation and the reports of neighbours. For the rest of her life she reverted for financial reasons to her English training in popular literature. She embarked on a series of highly romantic light novels that were far from reflecting the Canadian realities of the times.

The record of settlement in southern Ontario should be balanced by the contemporaneous *Winter Studies and Summer Rambles in Canada* (1838) by Anna Jameson, who explored what Europeans considered "the wilderness." Most of what is today called Canada was still the domain of the native peoples. It was known only to explorers, *voyageurs, coureurs de bois,* and the odd trader. Anna Jameson's curiosity helped her to know it too.

Anna Jameson visited Canada in 1836 at the request of her estranged husband, Robert Sympson Jameson, Upper Canada's first Attorney General, later Vice-Chancellor. She was already a literary success in England, as the author of the novel *The Diary of an Ennuyée.* She was also known for her *Characteristics of Women,* a work on Shakespeare's heroines seen from a woman's (almost a feminist's) point of view.

Winter Studies and Summer Rambles in Canada records her rather cold and dismal stay in Toronto where she had to play the role of wife, and her much livelier summer travelling. She set out

Mrs Jameson En Route for Lake Ontario 1835

"Mrs. Jameson En Route for Lake Ontario 1835"

across south-western Ontario and visited the new settlements. She went north by steamer from Detroit to the island of Michilimackinac, then on to Sault Ste Marie in a *bateau* powered by seven *voyageurs*. At the age of forty-three she shot the rapids there in a canoe:

> My Indians were enchanted, and when I reached *home,* my good friends were not less delighted at my exploit: they told me I was the first European female who had ever performed it, and assuredly I shall not be the last. I recommend it as an exercise before breakfast. Two glasses of champagne could not have made me more tipsy and more self-complacent!

"Home" was an Indian matriarch's house. Anna was made an honorary member of the family for this exploit.

She had the courage to go down Lake Huron in a canoe. She stopped at Manitoulin Island to observe the annual ceremony of gift-giving by British authorities to their Indian allies; three thousand seven hundred Indians were in attendance. After her return to Toronto, she did not stay long in Canada. Back in England, she continued to write and became a distinguished art critic and art historian.

Canadians remember Anna Jameson as the liveliest though not the last of the lady visitors.

A more "suitable" way for a lady to enjoy a canoe — used as a hammock (1850)

For Discussion

1. How is nature dealt with in Frances Brooke's *The History of Emily Montague* and Susanna Moodie's *Roughing It in the Bush?* What features of landscape and weather attract the authors? What features cause them the most difficulty and why?

2. Frances Brooke's first novel appeared anonymously, though her later work appeared under her own name. Why would she have published her first work anonymously? Why, in a later period, did Mary Ann Evans (George Eliot) in England and Aurore Lucie Dupin, Baroness Dudevant (Georges Sand) in France have their novels published under male pseudonyms?

3. Catherine Parr Traill's *The Backwoods of Canada* and Susanna Moodie's *Roughing It in the Bush* might be expected to be similar, as the authors were sisters and had similar experiences on arriving in Canada. What differences do you find in their accounts? What historical or personality factors give each book a distinctive tone?

4. What Europeans considered to be the wilderness had been inhabited for centuries by the native peoples. To them it was not a wilderness but a home. How much of a sense of this do you get from Susanna Moodie and Catherine Parr Traill, who lived near some Indian peoples? What are their attitudes to their neighbours?

   How different from these settlers' attitudes are those of Anna Jameson, in *Winter Studies and Summer Rambles?* How would you account for the difference?

5. Take a look at *A Gentlewoman in Upper Canada: The Journals of Anne Langton,* for its account of life in a pioneer settlement once the land is cleared and the farming well under way. In what ways was Anne Langton's life easier than Susanna Moodie's? Compare the activities in which they engaged.

For Research

Analyze similarities and differences in the portrayal of male and female roles in the writings of Susanna Moodie and Catherine Parr Traill. What assumptions about the proper roles of men and women are conveyed in these writings? How do these assumptions seem to have affected the goals and achievements of the men and women portrayed?

   Consider your own talents and interests. What opportunities would there have been for you had you lived in the era of Susanna Moodie and Catharine Parr Traill?

For Reading

Brooke, Frances. *The History of Emily Montague*. New Canadian Library #27. McClelland & Stewart, 1961.

Jameson, Anna. *Winter Studies and Summer Rambles in Canada: Selections*. New Canadian Library #26. McClelland & Stewart, 1965.

(Langton, Anne) *A Gentlewoman in Upper Canada: The Journals of Anne Langton,* ed. H. H. Langton. Clarke Irwin, 1950. Also in Clarke Irwin's Canadian Paperback Series, CI 3.

Moodie, Susanna. *Life in the Clearings,* ed. R. L. McDougall. Laurentian Library #39. Macmillan of Canada, 1976.

Moodie, Susanna. *Roughing It in the Bush*. New Canadian Library #31. McClelland & Stewart, 1962.

(Simcoe, Elizabeth) *Mrs. Simcoe's Diary,* ed. Mary Quayle Innis. Macmillan of Canada, 1965.

Traill, Catherine Parr. *The Backwoods of Canada*. New Canadian Library #51. McClelland & Stewart, 1966.

Traill, Catherine Parr. *The Canadian Settler's Guide*. New Canadian Library #64. McClelland & Stewart, 1969.

Klinck, C. F. "British in the Bush." *Canadian Literature,* no. 27 (Winter 1966) , 77-79. (Anna Jameson) .

Klinck, C. F. "A Gentlewoman of Upper Canada." *Canadian Literature,* no. 1 (Summer 1959) , 75-77. (Susanna Moodie) .

Morris, Audrey. *Gentle Pioneers: Five Nineteenth-Century Canadians*. Toronto: Hodder & Stoughton, 1968. Also in paperback: Paperjacks, General Publishing, 1973. (Susanna Moodie, Catherine Parr Traill)

New, William H. "Frances Brooke's Chequered Gardens." *Canadian Literature,* no. 52 (Spring 1972) , 24-38.

Thomas, Clara. "Journeys to Freedom." *Canadian Literature,* no. 51 (Winter 1972) , 11-19. (Susanna Moodie, Catherine Parr Traill, Anna Jameson)

Thomas, Clara. *Love and Work Enough: The Life of Anna Jameson*. University of Toronto Press, 1967.

Chapter 2

Towards a Canadian Literature

There is almost a full generation between the pioneer writers and visiting diarists, and the next group of women writers. During this time Canadian authors were turning from observation and description to more imaginative types of writing. Poems, short stories and novels were coming of age. In the early eighteen hundreds, book publishing was becoming a reality in Canada. The first novel published in Canada (Kingston, 1824) was by a woman, Julia Beckwith Hart. Her *St. Ursula's Convent, or, The Nun of Canada* was also the first novel by a native-born Canadian. During the second half of the nineteenth century the publishing industry in Canada was growing, and a Canadian writer no longer had to send manuscripts to London (or New York) to ensure publication.

The new nationalism of 1867 and the "Canada First" movement played their parts in developing a Canadian identity, but they should not be over-emphasized in the cultural history of the time. "Confederation" stopped at the western edge of Ontario, and it would take another generation for the western parts of British North America to join as provinces. The many and various ties with Britain were still overpowering influences on Canadian literature.

This can be seen in the writing of Isabella Valancy Crawford (1850-1887). When she was eight, her family moved to Canada from Ireland, and lived in a number of small towns. The family was beset by health and money problems. On her father's death, when she was twenty-five, Isabella was the only one of twelve children remaining. She and her mother moved to Toronto, and lived in great poverty. To support them, she wrote for the periodical market. A romantic at heart, her imagination was fired by stories of pioneering, travelling, cowboys, and the beginnings of North-West development.

Prose writings and journalism kept her alive, but she never became famous. In 1884 she published *Old Spookses' Pass, Malcolm's Katie, and Other Poems* at her own expense. Only fifty copies were sold. Three years later she died at the age of thirty-seven. *The Collected Poems of Isabella Valancy Crawford*, edited by J. W. Garvin, surfaced in Toronto in 1905 and started to earn posthumous recognition of her work.

Her graceful lyrics show her wide reading in other cultures — medieval, Greek and Oriental. Nevertheless, in her strongest work her romantic imagination fuses with her knowledge of Canadian scenes. For instance, "Old Spookses' Pass" is a Western dialect poem told from a cowboy's point of view. It is a vivid story which combines mountains, night, danger, a cattle stampede and an invisible night-rider into a "horror story" with a happy ending.

Her best-known poem is the long narrative "Malcolm's Katie." This is a vigorous tale of true and false love. Max is the heroic pioneer who sets out to clear a farm for Katie, and Alfred is the smooth hypocrite who sets out to win her in Max's absence. The

Isabella Valancy Crawford

romance ends happily after great trials of love for both Katie and
Max. It is not an artificial ending; it is prepared for in the very
opening of the poem by the description of the symbolic ring
which joins their initials.

> Max placed a ring on little Katie's hand,
> A silver ring that he had beaten out
> From that same sacred coin — first well prized wage
> For boyish labour, kept thro' many years.

In such poems, the work of Isabella Valancy Crawford has an
energy and vitality very different from the conditions of her own
grim urban life and depressed health.

Pauline Johnson (1861-1913) was to have the opposite fate —
personal success and fame — but little better luck in terms of
money. The first woman poet of note to be born in Canada, she
was the daughter of an Englishwoman and of a Mohawk leader
who had had an English education in Brantford. Home was a
place of culture, wide reading, and distinguished visitors. Her
father's death brought financial difficulties and the break-up of
the family when she was twenty-five. At this time she began
sending her poems to various periodicals.

Pauline Johnson

Two of her poems were selected for Lighthall's nationalistic
anthology, *Songs of the Great Dominion;* these were then singled
out for special praise by an eminent English critic in 1889.
However, 1892 was the real turning point in her career: a reading
of two dramatic poems at a concert in Toronto changed her from
a needy poet to a charismatic stage performer. Her first tour in
England was an unqualified success and she arranged to have her
poems published there (*The White Wampum*, 1895). In 1897
she joined forces with William McRaye, who did readings of
W. H. Drummond's *habitant* poems. McRaye carried much of the
burden of organizing concert tours, and he built up the "royal
princess" legends which began to surround Pauline Johnson
wherever she appeared. She was on the road as a touring
performer for twenty years.

A second volume, *Canadian Born* (1903), was somewhat
weaker than her first. Then her health began to break. She retired
in 1909 to Vancouver, where her friendship with Chief Joe
Capilano led her to write prose. Her versions of West Coast
Indian tales were first printed in the Vancouver *Province* and
then collected in book form as *Legends of Vancouver* (1911).
She was a writer of stories at this time, but knowing that she was
dying of cancer she collected her poems together in *Flint and
Feather* (1912).

Her reputation as a stage performer was more durable than her
reputation as a poet. Today her poems, especially "The Song My
Paddle Sings," are most often found in anthologies for children
and young people. Nevertheless, her gift for lyric verse is considerable. Her love of nature makes her Canadian wilderness into
an ally rather than an enemy. Insisting proudly on her Indian

Klootchman Indians at Fort St. James,
British Columbia, 1911

blood and heritage, she makes the "noble savage" the hero of her poems.

The romantic visions of Isabella Valancy Crawford and Pauline Johnson were well in tune with the literary tastes of the times in poetry. A different note — one of detached observation, humour and irony — came at much the same time, from the pen of a novelist born and raised in Brantford, Ontario. While much of Sara Jeannette Duncan's life and writings do not belong to Canadian history, she is associated with Canada for one of her novels in particular.

Sara Jeannette Duncan (1862-1922) was first a teacher and then a journalist. Her second career took her to the Memphis (Tennessee) *Appeal,* the Washington *Post,* the Toronto *Globe,* and as Parliamentary correspondent, to the Montreal *Star.* In 1891 she married Everard Cotes, the curator of the Indian Museum in Calcutta. She spent the rest of her life in India and England, writing a series of novels published in London or New York.

Her novels reflect her detached journalist's outlook, the foreign settings she knew from her many travels, and an implicit philosophy that "British" isn't necessarily "better." *The Imperialist* (Toronto and New York, 1904) is her "Canadian" novel, relying on her knowledge of Brantford and perhaps her Canadian newspaper work. The plot revolves around a naive young man who is a strong supporter of the Imperial Federation movement just when it is becoming a losing cause politically. There are a

Frontispiece and title page of Vernon's Aunt, *one of Sara Jeanette Duncan's novels*

KNOCKED HIM DOWN [p. 186]

VERNON'S AUNT

BEING THE

Oriental Experiences of Miss Lavinia Moffat

BY

SARA JEANNETTE DUNCAN

(MRS EVERARD COTES)

WITH 47 ILLUSTRATIONS BY HAL HURST

London
CHATTO & WINDUS, PICCADILLY
1894

number of romantic sub-plots. The core of the novel is its presentation of social tensions, especially between those who admire all things British and those who no longer do so. Referring to a recently arrived English gentleman,

> "I heard he was asking at Volunteer Headquarters the other night," remarked Alec, "how long it would be before a man like himself, if he threw in his lot with the country, could expect to get nominated for a provincial seat."
>
> "What did they tell him?" asked Mr Murchison, when they had finished their laugh.
>
> "I heard they said it would depend a good deal on the size of the lot."

In *The Imperialist* both private and public aspects of small town life are recorded with gentle criticism. In Sara Jeannette Duncan, Canada found its first native-born yet detached novelist.

It is tempting to speculate as to why in this generation married women tended to write novels and single women tended to write poetry. At any rate, the trend in poetry toward romantic vision continued. The best example in Canada is the work of Marjorie Pickthall during the first two decades of the twentieth century.

Born in England in 1883, Marjorie Pickthall came to Canada at the age of six. Shyness, poor health and a love of reading seemed to destine her to a life devoted to writing. Spurred on by success in poetry contests as a young woman, she wrote short stories, Indian legends, lyric poems, and children's literature. She sent them out to British and American as well as Canadian periodicals and met with appreciation on all sides. Her romantic and lyric tendency appealed to a world which did not want to know that it was headed for war.

After the death of her mother in 1910, she worked in a library until poor health made that impossible. She was convinced by friends and by her father (who later became her literary executor) to save all of her strength for writing. She went back to England for the best medical care, and stayed there for seven years. Before leaving Canada, she had been persuaded by scholars and critics to collect her poems into a book. *Drift of Pinions* (1913) was the result, with forty-three poems in praise of beauty, goodness, love, and the life of the spirit. In important ways this book is not "Canadian." It belongs to the country of the mind, of reading and ideas.

During the First World War, Marjorie Pickthall tried various kinds of war work, but her health did not allow her to keep them up. She retired to a cottage in the country, but constant writing did little for her recuperation. Influenced by the English Pre-Raphaelite Movement, the Irish Renaissance, and wanderers such as Robert Louis Stevenson and John Masefield, she continued to write lyric poems. These were added to the poems of her first collection and issued as *The Lamp of Poor Souls, and Other Poems* in 1916. At the same time she wrote more rugged and adventurous short stories and sold them to highly respected

Marjorie Pickthall

magazines such as *Harper's* and *Atlantic Monthly*. She also tried her hand, less successfully, at writing novels.

Homesick for Canada, she returned in 1920 and went to live in British Columbia, which until then had only been one of the lands of her dreams and her reading. When her health permitted, she would write. She made her favourite work, a poetic drama, the title piece of *The Woodcarver's Wife, and Later Poems*, published just before her early death in 1922. Her father collected the best of her short stories in *Angels' Shoes* (1923) and her poetry in *The Complete Poems of Marjorie Pickthall* (1925).

Her reputation has since been secured by the high level of craftsmanship in her work. She belongs with the last Romantics. A representative example of her imagery and atmosphere comes from "Vision," the very first poem in the *Complete Poems*:

> I have not walked on common ground,
> Nor drunk of earthly streams;
> A shining figure, mailed and crowned,
> Moves softly through my dreams.

Her poetry ranges as her reading did through history and geography at will. There is very little in it that can be recognized as Canadian, and this may have been a reason for its popularity.

The romantic lyric was to remain the poetic form for a while yet. Similarly, the Canadian novel had not yet begun to show any influence from European realism, or naturalism, or even from Sara Jeannette Duncan's witty objectivity. Romance and sentiment in their public and social forms were the staple of the novel.

The novels of Lucy Maud Montgomery (1874-1942) were romances of a kind, using local, Prince Edward Island settings and characters. L. M. Montgomery was raised by her grandparents and this upbringing was a key factor, not only in her desire to write, but also in the subject matter of her novels. Her own riotous love of life, nature and beauty was poured into her scribblers from childhood on. They were her way of coming to terms with living with stern grandparents and twice the usual generation gap. Her novels were to reflect, again and again, situations in which children grew up without one parent, or both, and fought restrictive forces.

As an adolescent, L. M. Montgomery wrote poems, short stories and children's magazine fare, sending them out to Canadian and then American periodicals. She became a teacher on the Island, and for a short time a journalist in Halifax. She was beginning to earn money from her magazine work. However, the main force in her life was her grandmother, and she returned home. Her grandfather was dead and she felt obliged to care for the woman who had raised her. She put off her own marriage until her grandmother's death in 1911.

During these years she would write every day. Slowly she earned both money and reputation. A long preparation in writing children's literature finally paid off in 1908, when she was thirty-three, with the publication and immediate international success

Lucy Maud Montgomery in 1908

of *Anne of Green Gables*. She had intended it for an adolescent audience and was surprised that many adults loved it. Mark Twain wrote her and praised it.

In *Anne of Green Gables* L. M. Montgomery captured the strong feelings and the trials and tribulations of childhood. The rest of her literary career was devoted (sometimes against the grain) to writing sequels, from *Anne of Avonlea* in 1909 to *Anne of Ingleside* in 1939. She created several other Prince Edward Island heroines; there are three Emily novels and two Pat novels. But the Island itself remained the "hero" of her work, even after she left it, following her marriage to the Reverend Ewen Macdonald.

She became a clergyman's wife and the mother of two sons as well as the inveterate scribbler. She also tried her hand at novels for adults (*The Blue Castle* and *A Tangled Web*), without much success. In spite of her popularity as a novelist she preferred to think of herself as a poet, and collected her poems into *The Watchman and Other Poems* (1917).

This cottage, where Maud lived with her grandmother, is often thought of as "Green Gables" although Maud never revealed the exact location of Anne's home.

At times, she actively disliked her steady production of young heroines. Her books sold well, but none recaptured the magic of the first one, *Anne of Green Gables,* with its humorous portrait of the red-haired orphan. The story may owe its popularity among adults to the fact that every reader can identify with Anne's provoking and provoked ways.

The other key to its success is L. M. Montgomery's rendering of Prince Edward Island. Landscape, sea and fresh air are not just a convenient background; they help Anne in her adjustment to a new family and environment.

> It was a September evening and all the gaps and clearings in the woods were brimmed up with ruby sunset light. Here and there the lane was splashed with it, but for the most part it was already quite shadowy beneath the maples . . . The cows swung placidly down the lane, and Anne followed them dreamily . . .

The dreadful pioneer "bush" is a long way back. Prince Edward Island has been tamed enough to become idyllic, and as such has close affinities with the rural Ontario of Stephen Leacock's *Sunshine Sketches of a Little Town.*

At much the same time that the Island and southern Ontario were becoming comfortable enough to be described in rural idylls, the West was being settled. The transcontinental railroad was finally completed in 1885. Various parts of the Prairies joined Confederation as provinces in their own right. Immigrants from all parts of Europe came to break the sod and farm the rich soil. Summers were intensely hot and winters intensely cold, but homesteaders continued to pour in. The movement was barely diverted by the gold rush of 1898 in the North-West.

Nellie McClung (1873-1951) was born in Ontario, and her family moved west to Manitoba on the strength of reports of good land. She grew up in relative poverty and had a scanty formal education — all that there was in a new farming community — but her strong and spirited personality carried her into a whole series of careers. She was a schoolteacher when she was in her teens. She became wife, mother of five children, novelist, temperance advocate, suffragist, lecturer, and member of the Alberta Legislature.

The humour, wit and vitality of Nellie McClung are revealed as much in her writing as in her political activities. She sent short stories to various publications, some of them temperance magazines. In 1908 she brought together a number of inter-related stories in *Sowing Seeds in Danny.* An international bestseller, it sold a hundred thousand copies. This first "novel" is roughly based on the author's life and acquaintances as a child in rural Manitoba. With considerable humour, she refashions events into romances and moral tales in which virtue inevitably triumphs.

Her own moral optimism and the popularity of sentimental and moralistic fiction guided the rest of her short story and novel writing. *Purple Springs* (1921) continues the story of Pearl

Mark Twain wrote me that in *Anne* I have created "the dearest, and most lovable child in fiction since the immortal Alice." Do you think I wasn't *proud* of Mark's encomium? Oh, perhaps not.

from a letter by Lucy Maud Montgomery

Nellie McClung

Watson, the twelve-year-old girl at the centre of *Sowing Seeds in Danny,* into a schoolteaching role and the questions and problems of women's rights. Moving outside her own experiences, Nellie McClung again dealt with women's roles in *Painted Fires* (1925), the story of a young Finnish immigrant girl.

In a sense her best writing is not in her short stories or novels at all. She turned to autobiography in *Clearing in the West: My Own Story* (1935). Here she was free of the moral and romantic conventions of fiction. *Clearing in the West* records her roots in Ontario, the move to the Red River, and the pioneer community. It also describes the social forces that she would rebel against. An enterprising woman who ran one of the "stopping houses" told her

> "If I weren't so busy feedin' hungry men and makin' bread and pies in my spare time, I could think out a few things. Maybe you'll do it sissy, when you grow up."
>
> "Maybe I will," I said eagerly, "I'd like to."
>
> When we were in the sleigh again, Mother told me I should not be so forward. It did not look well for a little girl to jump up and pour tea for strange men.

Clearing in the West, which takes Nellie to the time of her marriage, reveals how and why a bright girl with few chances in life became an evangelical and optimistic crusader for women's rights. The story of her life is continued in *The Stream Runs Fast* (1945), about her married life and her role as a political force in Manitoba and Alberta.

A Western homestead

1. How does Isabella Valancy Crawford's attitude about "the bush" in her poem "Malcolm's Katie" differ from that of Susanna Moodie in *Roughing It in the Bush*? What are some of the factors that might account for the difference?

2. Sara Jeanette Duncan's town of Elgin in *The Imperialist* and Frances Brooke's Quebec City in *The History of Emily Montague* are more than one hundred years apart. Are there many changes in the roles that women play in their respective communities? If so, what factors may account for the changes?

3. How different are Nellie McClung's versions of growing up in the West, in the fictional *Sowing Seeds in Danny*, and the auto-biographical *Clearing in the West*?

4. To what extent were the views expressed by Nellie McClung in her novels consistent with those she expressed as a political activist?

The creative process is — depending on which author you ask — anything from mysterious to prosaic. L. M. Montgomery has left letters and articles describing her creative life in some depth. Report on *The Green Gable Letters* (Ryerson Press, 1960) and *The Alpine Path: The Story of My Career* (Fitzhenry and Whiteside, 1974). What light do they shed on your reading of *Anne of Green Gables*? What light do they shed on the problems of being a Canadian author?

What aspects of Indian life are touched on in Pauline Johnson's poems? How close does her portrayal of the Indian come to the stereotype of the "noble savage"? Discuss whether you think this had a bearing on the fact that she made her living by reading her poetry in an era when the native peoples were largely mis-understood.

How does Marjorie Pickthall's "Père Lalement" (one of her few distinctly Canadian poems) depict the relationship of the mis-sionary to the native peoples? What has she chosen to emphasize? What has she omitted? What effect does this selection process have on your sympathies for both the priest and the Indians?
From library sources available to you, investigate the treatment of early missionaries by the Indians in various kinds of historical records. How does "Père Lalement" compare?

For Reading

Crawford, Isabella Valancy. *The Collected Poems of Isabella Valancy Crawford,* ed. J. G. Garvin, 1905, reprinted with an introduction by James Reaney. Literature of Canada: Poetry and Prose in Reprint. University of Toronto Press, 1972.

Crawford, Isabella Valancy. *Selected Stories,* ed. Penny Petrone. University of Ottawa Press, 1975.

Duncan, Sara Jeannette. *The Imperialist.* New Canadian Library #20. McClelland & Stewart, 1961.

Johnson, E. Pauline. *Legends of Vancouver.* McClelland & Stewart, 1961.

Johnson, E. Pauline. *Pauline Johnson: Her Life and Works,* ed. Marcus Van Steen. Musson, 1965.

McClung, Nellie. *Clearing in the West.* Thomas Allen, 1965.

McClung, Nellie. *Sowing Seeds in Danny.* Thomas Allen, 1965.

Montgomery, L. M. *Anne of Green Gables.* Ryerson Press, 1968.

Montgomery, L. M. *The Alpine Path: The Story of My Career.* Fitzhenry & Whiteside, 1974.

(Pickthall, Marjorie) *The Selected Poems of Marjorie Pickthall,* ed. Lorne Pierce. McClelland & Stewart, 1957.

Benham, Mary Lile. *Nellie McClung.* Fitzhenry & Whiteside, 1975.

Gerson, Carole. "Duncan's Web." *Canadian Literature,* no. 63 (Winter 1975), 73-80. (Sara Jeannette Duncan)

Gillen, Mollie. *The Wheel of Things: A Biography of L. M. Montgomery, Author of Anne of Green Gables.* Fitzhenry & Whiteside, 1975.

Livesay, Dorothy. "Tennyson's Daughter or Wilderness Child? The Factual and the Literary Background of Isabella Valancy Crawford." *Journal of Canadian Fiction,* vol. 2 (Summer 1973), 161-167.

Ower, John B. "Isabella Valancy Crawford: The Canoe." *Canadian Literature,* no. 34 (Autumn 1967), 54-62.

R., M. E. "Sara Jeannette Duncan: Personal Glimpses." *Canadian Literature,* no. 27 (Winter 1966), 15-19.

Reaney, James. "Isabella Valancy Crawford," in *Our Living Tradition,* Second and Third Series, ed. R. L. McDougall. University of Toronto Press, 1959.

Shrive, Norman. "What Happened to Pauline?" *Canadian Literature,* no. 13 (Summer 1962), 25-38.

The Tradition in Fiction

Women writers who came to fame during the nineteen twenties and thirties were facing a new world. The First World War had shocked a nation accustomed to peaceful political evolution. The international events in the following years indicated that the war had not guaranteed democracy or peace. The economic depression of the thirties hit Canada very hard. While women had received the vote and occupations were slowly opening to them, married women whose husbands had jobs were dismissed. Engaging in the act of writing was almost a luxury during those years.

Mazo de la Roche

*David Schurmann as Philip I and
Eve Crawford as Young Adeline I
in the CBC-TV series based on the
Jalna novels*

International trends in literature took a long time to permeate Canada. The new hard-edged images in poetry were not "beautiful" to readers raised on vague romantic lyrics. The realistic novel, a staple in France for fifty years, was rarely published in a land where Victorian sensibilities still operated — especially in the realm of fiction. The older voices, those of romance, remained side by side with newer ones.

Mazo de la Roche, one of the newer voices, became Canada's most famous novelist in the late twenties. She was born in 1879 and was thus a contemporary of L. M. Montgomery and Nellie McClung. Although she attended the Ontario College of Art, she wanted to be a writer. During her youth she sent stories out for magazine publication. She was often sick, there were many family illnesses and there were money problems. Life was better when the family moved out of Toronto to a country fruit farm, and (more important for her fiction later) she got to know and enjoy the rural landscape.

In 1915 her father died, and she moved back to Toronto and poverty. She also had her first acceptance of a story by the highly-respected *Atlantic Monthly*. She was thirty-six years old. She continued to write and sell short stories. In 1923 her first novel was published. *Possession* is no rural idyll; it is about the downfall of two men, an unbusinesslike gentleman-farmer, and a young architect forced to marry the Indian woman who has borne his child. While it is not exactly a realistic novel, it leans in that direction much more than the usual rural novel of the day.

Her second novel, *Delight* (1926), depicts life in a small town, especially the exuberant life of the main character, Delight Mainprize, the immigrant girl who works in a hotel. In these two novels one of Mazo de la Roche's main themes, the power of passion, got her into trouble with some Toronto-based reviewers. She commented bitterly, "Pity the Canadian novelist who does not write of the Woolly West or sweet 'homey' tales."

When success finally came in 1927 it came "overnight" and not from a Canadian source. She learned of a novel contest sponsored by the prestigious *Atlantic Monthly*. Macmillan in Toronto were arranging to publish her novel, *Jalna*, and let her submit it to the competition. She took first place and the ten-thousand-dollar prize. Her days of poverty were over.

She began writing a sequel, *Whiteoaks of Jalna*, which was published in 1929, and continued to write further sequels until the last one, *Morning at Jalna*, appeared in 1960. The series became a sixteen-volume saga of five generations of the Whiteoak family. She spent most of the years from 1929 to 1939 in England, returning to Canada because of the war. She wrote plays; she dramatised *Whiteoaks* for the stage. She wrote novels for children, and some serious novels about childhood and early environment. Late in life, she wrote her autobiography, *Ringing the Changes* (1957). She died in 1961 at the age of eighty-two.

Her international reputation is based on the *Jalna* series. The hundred years of family saga begin when Adeline Whiteoak with her soldier husband and first child come to Canada and take up a thousand acres in southern Ontario. They build a great house, Jalna, the focal point for all family members no matter how scattered. From the middle of the nineteenth century to the Second World War and beyond, there are family quarrels, loves, and hatreds. Beyond the human drama, the estate, as it passes from one generation to another, is an important "character." It comes to stand for the spirit of the most vivid character, Adeline Whiteoak, the quintessential matriarch.

Mazo de la Roche has been criticized by those who expected her work to develop toward rather than away from realism. But her efforts in that direction went unappreciated at the time. She was well past the middle of her life when she found her ideal recipe for fiction in *Jalna*, using her historical imagination and creating dramatic romances. Her *Jalna* protagonists are more Anglo-Irish than Canadian, and at the landed-gentry level of society. The day of the ordinary Canadian as hero would have to wait.

Another older voice belongs to Emily Carr (1871-1945). She did not write until late in life nor see any work published until she was seventy, and her writing has a flavour all of its own. She is not in the mainstream of literary trends or popular tastes affecting other writers. She was first of all a painter; writing was her second career. Her writings are essentially short sketches, impressions of

Once again a Canadian novelist has had to await recognition abroad in order to win appreciation at home. ... Now [Canadians] are applauding [Mazo de la Roche], not because her earlier books possess subtle merits, but because the Boston *literati* have decided that *Jalna* is worth $10,000.

from The Canadian Forum, *1927*

Emily Carr

Paintings by Emily Carr. Top:
Totem Poles at Kitseukla, *1911.*
Bottom: Big Raven, *1928*

her life and the various environments she lived in, always from her sensitive and rebellious viewpoint.

Emily Carr was born into a very British family in Victoria, B.C. She took art training in San Francisco, London and Paris, between bouts of work to support herself and painting trips to West Coast Indian settlements. She also suffered several severe illnesses. Carr had her first major art exhibition in 1911, when she was forty. Her work was ridiculed, and the same happened with her second exhibition in 1913. She ceased her trips to Indian outposts, and stopped painting.

Money was a constant problem for Emily Carr. She became a landlady; she raised sheep dogs for sale. Finally in 1927 (just when she was starting to write) she was recognized as a great modern Canadian painter by the National Gallery of Canada and her work was shown in its major exhibition of West Coast art. She went back to painting, leaving the Indian themes and concentrating on the great forests. Heart trouble dogged her, but while she was recuperating, she would write and revise.

Her first book, *Klee Wyck,* came out in 1941, just before her seventieth birthday. This collection of stories concerning her early visits to remote Indian settlements was a great success, and won the Governor General's award for general literature. By the end of 1942, she had put together *The Book of Small,* probably her best-loved book. The first half deals with her earliest memories and experiences of life. Into it she pours all of the joys and frustrations of being a small rebel in a large family, and writes of her great love for animals and the outdoors. The second half describes the slow, steady growth of Victoria from its start as a sleepy little place where cows could freely browse.

The House of All Sorts (1944) records her trials as a landlady during the long years when she was bedevilled by cranky roomers, lack of money and house repair problems. It is enlivened by descriptions of her well-loved dogs and her passion for her garden. By this time she had also completed her autobiography, *Growing Pains,* but insisted that it could not be published until she died. Sales of both paintings and books finally relieved her of her financial worries before she died in 1945.

Growing Pains (1946) takes her from her baptism at the age of four to her old age. The highlights are descriptions of her travels, her art education, and the few people who became close friends. Most of it is devoted, as the title indicates, to "growing." There is little in it about the period after her return to Canada in 1911. Posthumous publication continued: *Pause* (1953), though written late in life, is about her eighteen months in an English sanatorium, cheered only by her attempt to raise songbirds. *The Heart of a Peacock* (1953), mostly written earlier, is a miscellaneous collection of stories and impressions of birds, Indians, her pet monkey Woo, and other favourite animals.

Her artist's notebook was her last book, and in some ways the best. *Hundreds and Thousands: The Journals of Emily Carr*

(1966) reveals her solitary, probing genius and her struggle to express nature in all its immensity and spirit. As a book, it is both more personal and more intellectual than her autobiographical sketches.

> Did good work this morning. Did poor work this afternoon. I am looking for something indescribable, so light it can be crushed by a heavy thought, so tender even our enthusiasm can wilt it, as mysterious as tears.

The writings of Emily Carr must have seemed to many to be a voice of the past in the nineteen forties, for a more modern voice had already been heard, in 1925. That year stands out as a landmark in the history of the Canadian novel for Martha Ostenso's *Wild Geese* and Frederick Philip Grove's *Settlers of the Marsh.* These novels are at the forefront of North American realism, in the same generation as Sherwood Anderson's *Winesburg, Ohio* (1919) and Sinclair Lewis' *Main Street* (1920). However, Canadian readers raised on *Sunshine Sketches,* Nellie McClung and L. M. Montgomery were not prepared to enjoy novels which concentrated on the darker side of rural life.

Martha Ostenso (1900-1963) was born in Norway and her family emigrated to the western United States when she was young. They settled in Brandon, Manitoba when she was a teenager. She went on to the University of Manitoba, and at seventeen spent a summer in northern Manitoba as a teacher. Here she met the environment that became the setting for *Wild Geese.* She went to Columbia University for a creative writing course, and started to write her novel. She sent a revision to the literary competition sponsored by the Famous Players — Lasky Corporation, which offered a $13,500 prize. *Wild Geese* took first place, which guaranteed publication, in 1925, a year or so before Mazo de la Roche won the *Atlantic Monthly* prize.

Frederick Philip Grove

Martha Ostenso may very well have been thought of by Canadians as an American. She remained in the United States and wrote over a dozen novels, usually set in the American Mid-West, and published in New York. Nevertheless, *Wild Geese* should be considered as a Canadian novel of the new frontier of the day: once the southern part of the Prairies was tamed, the geographical boundary between man and unclaimed land moved northwards.

Wild Geese is primarily the story of a harsh and cruel farmer, Caleb Gare. He is obsessed with the success of his farming and he would sacrifice his wife and three children if need be. The novel is told mainly from the point of view of a young visiting teacher who boards at the farmhouse. Her first impression of Caleb is hardly alleviated by the forewarning words of his rebellious daughter:

Martha Ostenso

> "You might as well know that he'll try to bully you," she said matter-of-factly. "He's starting by keeping supper waiting . . . He expects you to be a man. All the teachers have been men. He's in for a jolt. But you stick up for yourself, Miss Archer. Don't let him bully you."

Though there are two love stories in the novel, there is little sentimentality. Love is a life force contrasted with the negative forces that Caleb represents. Finally the daughter gets away, Caleb nearly kills his wife for letting her do so, and then is killed himself while trying to save his precious flax crop from fire.

This powerful novel, with its focus on the dark side of human nature, could not by itself bring Canadian literature into the camp of the realists. However, it showed what use could be made of really difficult struggles among people, and between people and landscape. Henceforth, realism in setting if not in plot would be a growing force in the novel.

A good case in point is the Manitoba-based work of Laura Goodman Salverson (1890-1970). Of Icelandic parentage, she grew up on both sides of the Western border as a member of an immigrant wave (only one of many in the development of the West) that was not always made to feel welcome. Her father, something of a poet and intellectual, had to work as a cobbler in Winnipeg for twelve to fourteen hours a day, merely to put bread on the table. Spurred by her father's example of writing for Icelandic journals late at night, Laura turned to writing lyric poems and novels.

Winnipeg slums, 1930s

Her first and most successful novel, *The Viking Heart,* was published in 1933. It describes realistically the great hardships experienced by poor Icelandic settlers who came to Manitoba after the massive volcanic eruptions in Iceland in 1876. It also contains a number of romantic stories in which love and devotion can usually overcome the tragedies brought on by poverty, hard labour, crop failure and mental illness.

Her second novel, *When Sparrows Fall* (1925), deals with the life of second-generation Scandinavian settlers in the western United States. Further novels were historical romances based on the Icelandic history and legends she had absorbed, as a sickly child, from her parents. Then, in 1937, she won the Governor General's award for *The Dark Weaver.* In this novel she returns to the Manitoba setting, and to her observations of the life of the Icelandic immigrant. It is a much sadder novel than *The Viking Heart,* at times bitter:

> No understanding these things really. Neither justice nor virtue had any part in this tangled web of human destinies — curious diablerie of an inscrutable Weaver!

The Dark Weaver is particularly sensitive about the oppression of wives, either emotionally through ill-matched husbands, or biologically through yearly unwanted babies. It ends tragically when the best of the second generation, ironically well-matched, both die in the First World War far away from home.

Her next book also won a Governor General's award, but not for fiction. *Confessions of an Immigrant's Daughter* (1939) is her autobiography up to the age of thirty-three, that is, the years until *The Viking Heart* was published. It reveals the grinding poverty of immigrants, the sweatshop conditions in Winnipeg under which her father had to work, and his various flights to better his lot both in Canada and the United States. It also reveals Laura Goodman Salverson's courage and determination as she went from miserable job to miserable job as a young woman, then shared a life of poverty with her husband in the Canadian West, as she struggled to become an author. Her mother had taught her well.

> But grief, like everything else, was a luxury, mother told herself harshly. There was no time for tears. She had work to find — any kind of work. And how gladly she toiled! How proudly and gratefully she counted each dollar that, bit by bit, would cancel those intolerable obligations.

The fiction and non-fiction work of Laura Goodman Salverson is a useful corrective to the usual Anglo-Canadian middle-class bias in much of our early literature. She and Martha Ostenso wrote realistically about successful Canadians in their worst light, as tyrants over the poor and powerless.

A recently arrived group of immigrants in front of the CPR station in Winnipeg, 1907

For Discussion

1. Susanna Moodie's *Roughing It in the Bush* is at times a very stark account of emigration and settling. How different is Mazo de la Roche's account of rural establishment in *Jalna*? What problems does Mazo de la Roche ignore? Why? To what effect?

2. A non-British immigrant was often less acceptable than a British one. Whether you had money or not was also an important factor, as the career of Emily Carr's father shows. What differences are there in opportunities for immigrants in Emily Carr's *The Book of Small* (and early parts of *Growing Pains*) , and in Laura Goodman Salverson's *Confessions of an Immigrant's Daughter*? To what extent was being a woman a factor in being able to take advantage of opportunities?

3. The province of Manitoba reaches northward from the forty-ninth parallel. How far north you are has important effects on climate, soil, and plant life. In what ways is rural life similar in Nellie McClung's *Sowing Seeds in Danny* and Martha Ostenso's *Wild Geese*? In what ways are their representations of rural Manitoba different?

For Research

Emily Carr was both painter and author. Reproductions of her paintings can be seen in the Vancouver Art Gallery's 1971 catalogue, *Emily Carr: A Centennial Exhibition*. Report on the correspondences between its photographs of her paintings and her notebook entries in *Hundreds and Thousands*.

Interview some recent men and women immigrants in your community. What attracted them to Canada? How much culture shock did they experience on arrival? What are their ambitions and goals, and are there any obstacles? Are there any similarities or differences between the experiences of men and women?

If your community is urban, compare their experiences with those of the Icelanders in Laura Goodman Salverson's *The Viking Heart* or *Confessions of an Immigrant's Daughter*. If your community is rural, compare their experiences with those of the various immigrants in Susanna Moodie's *Roughing It in the Bush,* or Nellie McClung's *Clearing in the West,* or Martha Ostenso's *Wild Geese*.

For Reading

Carr, Emily. *The Book of Small*. Canadian Paperback CI 20.
    Clarke Irwin, 1966.
Carr, Emily. *Growing Pains: The Autobiography of Emily
    Carr*. Canadian Paperback CI 24. Clarke Irwin, 1966.
Carr, Emily. *Klee Wyck*. Canadian Paperback CI 9. Clarke
    Irwin, 1965.
De la Roche, Mazo. *Delight*. New Canadian Library #21.
    McClelland & Stewart, 1961.
De la Roche, Mazo. *Jalna*. The entire series in Pan or Macmillan
    paperback.
Ostenso, Martha. *Wild Geese*. New Canadian Library #18.
    McClelland & Stewart, 1961.
Salverson, Laura Goodman. *Confessions of an Immigrant's
    Daughter*. Ryerson Press, 1939.
Salverson, Laura Goodman. *The Viking Heart*. New Canadian
    Library #116. McClelland & Stewart, 1975.

Daniells, Roy. "Emily Carr," in *Our Living Tradition,* Fourth
    Series, ed. R. L. McDougall. University of Toronto Press, 1962.
Hambleton, Ronald. *Mazo de la Roche of Jalna*. General
    Publishing, 1966.
Hendrick, George. *Mazo de la Roche*. Twayne's World Authors.
    Boston: Twayne, 1970.
McCourt, Edward A. "Laura Goodman Salverson," in his *The
    Canadian West in Fiction*. Ryerson Press, 1970.
Smith, Marion. "Period Pieces." *Canadian Literature,* no. 10
    (Autumn 1961) , 72-77. (Martha Ostenso)
Thomas, Clara. "Martha Ostenso's Trial of Strength," in *Writers
    of the Prairies,* ed. D. G. Stephens. Canadian Literature Series.
    University of British Columbia Press, 1973.
Tippett, Maria. "Emily Carr's *Klee Wyck*." *Canadian
    Literature,* no. 72 (Spring 1977) , 49-58.

Chapter 4

New Waves in Poetry

T. S. Eliot

F. R. Scott

A. J. M. Smith

After the First World War, Canadian poetry began to reflect new trends in international literary circles. The era of sentimental and visionary verse was waning. Around 1925 poets like A. J. M. Smith and F. R. Scott brought a new toughness, intellectuality, and a high level of craftsmanship into their poetry. Some were influenced by the "imagist" movement in Britain and the United States, and concentrated on precise and vivid images. Others followed in the wake of T. S. Eliot and wrote allusive, cryptic poems critical of the contemporary scene. The subject matter of poetry in Canada was at last enlarged beyond the usual perimeter of love — for God, for country, for the maple, for human beings.

Over a span of fifty years, Dorothy Livesay (born 1909) has usually been at the forefront of successive waves of new influences. Raised in Winnipeg and then Toronto, she studied at the University of Toronto and then spent a year at the Sorbonne in Paris in 1932. By this time she was a published poet. *Green Pitcher* (1928) contains short lyrics mainly in the imagist tradition. *Signpost* (1932) is more personal, deeply concerned with human emotions.

In Paris, she was involved with a League of Revolutionary Writers and began to write from a socialist standpoint. Her concern for the poor during the Depression was not confined to her poetry. She returned to Toronto and took her diploma in social work in 1934. Her career as a social worker took her to Quebec, New Jersey, and then British Columbia in 1936. Her knowledge of and sympathy with the oppressed led her to produce mostly "agit-prop" plays, poems and speeches, intended for immediate political persuasion.

While in New Jersey, Dorothy Livesay became acquainted with the new poetry from Britain. The disillusionment of a T. S. Eliot seemed a dead end to young revolutionary writers. New inspiration came from Auden and Spender, who were able to write with hope from a left-wing position. In the midst of the Depression, she wrote what she has called her first "distanced" poem of the worker's life, "Day and Night." With its jazz rhythms and racial themes reminiscent of her days in New Jersey, and its sketches of the Canadian industrial scene, it is a revolutionary poem indeed.

> Men in a stream, a moving human belt
> Move into sockets, every one a bolt.
> The fun begins, a humming, whirring drum —
> Men do a dance in time to the machines.
>
> One step forward
> Two steps back
> Shove the lever,
> Push it back

In 1937 she married and made Vancouver her home. Here she raised a son and a daughter. "Day and Night" was written by

Dorothy Livesay

Japanese-Canadians on their way to internment camps in the B.C. interior, 1942

1936, but it was not published until 1940. Then it became the title poem of her 1944 volume of poems, *Day and Night,* which won the Governor General's award. This was followed by *Poems for People* (1947), which won the same award. These poems combine social concern with more personal humanism, especially in the "Poems for People" section. A mother's interest is apparent in the "Poems of Childhood." In 1947 she also received the Lorne Pierce medal from the Royal Society of Canada for distinguished contribution to Canadian literature.

During the next ten years she worked at a variety of careers — extension work, lecturing in creative writing, and adult and high school teaching. In 1949, she edited and wrote the introduction to *The Collected Poems of Raymond Knister.* In 1950 she published *Call My People Home,* a long documentary poem (written for radio) about the Japanese-Canadians interned in British Columbia after Japan bombed Pearl Harbor.

New Poems (1955) and *Selected Poems: 1926-1956* (1957) furthered her reputation as a perceptive lyric poet. Then in 1958, after twenty-two years in Vancouver, she went on her travels again, to London and then Paris. Widowed, she spent three years in Zambia (then Northern Rhodesia) teaching English for UNESCO. Her impressions of African people were worked into *The Colour of God's Face* (1964), later re-titled "Zambia." She

The second issue of CV II

returned to Vancouver, as a teaching assistant and then lecturer in creative writing.

In 1967 Dorothy Livesay broke new ground again with *The Unquiet Bed*. While this book contains longer poems, the section that gave the book its title is devoted to a frank exploration of physical love from the woman's point of view. These lyrics are not particularly reflective of the feminist movement as a social force, as they seem intensely personal.

In 1968 she collected together some of her longer poems into *The Documentaries,* bringing back into print the early, revolutionary "Day and Night" and "The Outrider." Not one to retire in any sense, she had embarked in 1966 on a career as writer-in-residence at the University of New Brunswick. This appointment was followed by others all over Canada. Her lyrical bent dominated her reflective and documentary side in *Plainsongs* (1969; extended issue, 1971) . In 1971, she edited an anthology of recent poems by *Forty Women Poets of Canada*. In 1972, she put together her own massive *Collected Poems: The Two Seasons*.

Nor is poetry her only medium. Stories written from the fifties onward appeared in *A Winnipeg Childhood* (1973, reissued in 1976 as *Beginnings*). These sketches about growing up are oddly reminiscent of Emily Carr's recapturings of early innnocence and childhood associations. Then Dorothy Livesay returned to her poetry with *Ice Age* (1975) , poems mainly concerning the theme of growing old. She has started a review of poetry, *CV/II* (named in honour of Vancouver's *Contemporary Verse,* which ran from 1941 to 1952) .

The accomplishment of Dorothy Livesay is impressive. Her early imagism has never quite died, as her apt brief descriptions still show. Her early love of nature, people, life itself, has not lessened. Beside a motel she finds an old apple tree and picks up an apple:

> In fifty seconds, fifty summers sweep
>   and shake me —
> I am alive! can stand
>   up still
> hoarding this apple
>   in my hand.

The poem is humorously entitled "Eve."

Many of Dorothy Livesay's poems had first been printed in little poetry magazines which flourished especially in the nineteen forties. These included *Preview, First Statement, Contemporary Verse,* and later *Northern Review*. Among the younger poets published in them were the "Forties" women poets. Something of the temper of the times can be seen in the early work of Anne Marriott, P. K. Page, and Miriam Waddington. It is noticeably left-wing, socially oriented, and the language is closer to that of ordinary people.

Anne Marriott (born 1913)   is from the West Coast. Her early work appeared in periodicals in the thirties. *The Wind Our Enemy* (1939) , only eight pages long, received a great deal of attention. Since then, it has appeared in many anthologies. She evokes the plight of westerners in the drought-ridden Prairies during the worst of the Depression.

> Wind
> filling the dry mouth with bitter dust
> whipping the shoulders worry-bowed too soon,
> soiling the water pail, and in grim prophecy
> greying the hair.

Realistic and imagistic description is interspersed with dialogue in the rhythms of normal workaday speech. What Dorothy Livesay had said for the urban worker in "Day and Night," Anne Marriott said for the poor farmer.

Another brief book, *Calling Adventures!* won the Governor General's award in 1941. It consists of the verse choruses of a radio documentary on Canada's North. *Salt Marsh and Other Poems* (1942) and *Sandstone and Other Poems* (1945) show further developments of her social concern and descriptive styles. These were her last books for a long time, as she was involved in a number of careers — editor of a verse column, co-founder of *Contemporary Verse* along with Dorothy Livesay, scriptwriter for the National Film Board, wife, mother, journalist, and librarian. During these years she continued to publish in periodicals, and wrote many CBC radio scripts. In 1971 she published another booklet, *Countries,* about the countries of the mind rather than geography. But *The Wind Our Enemy* remains Anne Marriott's outstanding work for its unsentimental portrayal of the Prairie drought and dust-storms.

Anne Marriott

Parched plains in Manitoba in the drought of the 1930s

P. K. Page

The Tamarack Review *publishes
the work of many Canadian poets.*

SUMMER 1976

The Tamarack Review

ISSUE 69

P.K. Page (born 1916) was born in England but came to Canada as a youngster and grew up on the Prairies. She started to write during the thirties, supporting herself by odd jobs in the Maritimes and Montreal, then the poetry centre of Canada. She became associated with the *Preview* group as editor. She was one of the five published in *Unit of Five* in 1944. In the same year, under the pseudonym "Judith Cape", she published a short novel, *The Sun and the Moon,* a psychological romance about a young woman with strange powers. Her first book of poems on her own is *As Ten As Twenty* (1946). These poems show a sympathetic concern for the lonely and powerless, although not from a doctrinaire socialist position. The book includes what is probably her best-known poem, "The Stenographers":

> In the felt of the morning the calico-minded,
> sufficiently starched, insert papers, hit keys,
> efficient and sure as their adding machines;
> yet they weep in the vault, they are taut as net curtains
> stretched upon frames.

From 1946 to 1950 P.K. Page was a scriptwriter for the National Film Board. In 1950 she married a Canadian diplomat and turned to a second career as a painter, under the name P.K. Irwin. During the fifties and sixties she lived in Australia, the United States, Brazil and Mexico as well as in Canada. Her second book of poems, *The Metal and the Flower* (1954), won the Governor General's award. It reveals again her concern for other people, as well as an interest in subjective processes and dreams.

In 1967 she collected those earlier poems that she wanted to preserve, and seventeen new ones, in *Cry Ararat!* Newer poems deal with landscapes, dreams, and states of childhood. The social critic is not asleep, however, in poems such as "On Educating the Natives":

> They who can from palm leaves and from grasses
> weave baskets of so intricate a beauty
> and simply as a girl combing her hair,
> are taught in a square room by a square woman
> to cross-stitch on checked gingham.

Her early novel and her short stories were reissued in 1973 as *The Sun and the Moon and Other Fictions.* Her latest collection of poetry, *Poems Selected and New* (1974) adds to her reputation for precise and original imagery, and her ability to evoke both pleasant and unpleasant psychological states. They also reflect her reactions to living in other cultures, and her later life in British Columbia.

Miriam Waddington (born 1917) is another poet associated with left-wing political philosophy. Born in Winnipeg and educated there and in Toronto, she became a social worker and worked in Ontario, Pennsylvania, and Quebec. In Montreal, she was associated with John Sutherland's *First Statement* group. Her first poems in book form were published by the First Statement Press in 1945 as *Green World.* The world of the poems is "green" in the sense of freshness, joy, and tenderness. Some are personal, while others are descriptive of the city and the lives of other people.

The Second Silence (1955) and *The Season's Lovers* (1958) carry on her work as a lyric poet. The first has poems about love, children and work. Some are shaped by her experiences as a wife and mother of two sons, others by her vision of the world in terms of summer and greenness — even in large cities. *The Season's Lovers* contains poems about urban life and its losers, perhaps a reflection of her Russian-socialist-Jewish background. It also has a number of powerful lyrics about love.

In 1963 Miriam Waddington left her first career as a social worker for her second as teacher, scholar and critic at York University. *The Glass Trumpet* (1966) and *Say Yes* (1969) show new interests. Some poems reflect travels in Europe, Russia and Israel, others her teaching of English and the writing of poetry. She also investigates her Jewish heritage and her life as a Prairie girl. In Russia, once the home of her immigrant parents, she feels alien, and in Jerusalem, even more so:

> I am homesick I
> am packing up
> I am going home
> but now I don't
> know anymore
> where home is.

The lines in the poems tend to be shorter, and the structure freer, than in the earlier poetry. The various subjects are still perceived by an affirmative, passionately involved personality.

Miriam Waddington's scholarly interest in Canadian literature and an old friendship with her first editor led her to edit *John Sutherland: Essays, Poems, Controversies* (1972). In 1973 she brought together a collection of her poems, *Driving Home: Poems New and Selected*. In it she deals with Canadian questions,

Men think I write about love and loss and flowers. They find it hard to accept the fact that women have ideas. I think I write poetry about the changing Canadian myth, I am a nationalist. I feel very close to the landscape. My new poetry is about space.

Miriam Waddington, in Merle Shain, "Some of our Best Poets Are . . . Women," Chatelaine, October, 1972

Miriam Waddington

Jewish heritage, and her wide-ranging sense of time. Her Jewish-Canadian interests can also be seen in her editing of *The Collected Poems of A.M. Klein* (1974) . Her most recent book of poems, *The Price of Gold* (1976) , shows her striding into the future, living alone, teaching, and facing up to the theme of death in poems about her dead ex-husband.

Her poems about ordinary Canadians, from hospital birth to rocking-chair old age, have been used as the text of a National Film Board book of black-and-white photographs, *Call Them Canadians* (1968) . Miriam Waddington's poems are notable for their immediacy, their vitality, and their unsentimental love of a country seen more as an urban than a rural environment.

Margaret Avison (born 1918) completes this group of poets coming to notice in the forties. Born in Galt, Ontario, she has been associated with Toronto since her undergraduate days. She worked for the University of Toronto, and later for Gage Publishing, for whom she wrote a young people's *History of Ontario* in 1951.

Her first poems did not appear in the left-wing periodicals, but rather in *Contemporary Verse* and the more general journal of Canadian thought and letters, the *Canadian Forum*. Later she published in American outlets such as the *Kenyon Review, Poetry* (Chicago) , and *Origin*. Her small output was respected for its search for meaning and its uncompromising perception of the world.

Her first book, *Winter Sun* (1960) , won the Governor General's award. It offers a keen vision of life in the city, rootless, bleak, and remote. It is a world of brooders and doubters. Her second book, *The Dumbfounding* (1966) , is a striking contrast to the first. Her inner quest has ended in a full acceptance of Christianity and many of the poems are celebrations of spiritual life. The language is contemporary and the rhythms are lyrical. Toronto offers even in small ways something to sing about, in spring:

> The grackle shining in long grass
> this first day of green casts
> an orchid-mile of shadow
> into the sun-meld, that marvel, those
> meadows of peace (between the bird
> and the curved curb
> of the city-center clover-leaf) .

During the sixties, Margaret Avison applied herself to graduate studies and taught at the University of Toronto. In 1968 she began a new career as a social worker for a Toronto Presbyterian mission. Thus she has come to social work not from the left-wing political framework that inspired Dorothy Livesay and Miriam Waddington, but from religious conviction.

These women poets who brought modern concerns and language into their work have done much to free poetry from narrow definitions and expectations. For the first time, urban life

[Margaret Avison's] poems are often about the love of God, as she was converted to Christianity at age forty-five. Reading the Bible one day she came across a verse in St. John, 14, which said: "Ye believe in God, believe also in me," and she said, "All right, I will, but you can't have my poetry." And then all at once she threw the Bible across the room and said, "All right take my poetry too."

from Merle Shain, "Some of Our Best Poets Are . . . Women," Chatelaine, *October, 1972*

in Canada is adequately presented. All of the problems of life, biological, economic, physical, spiritual, as well as romantic, become legitimate subject matter. There are tight, vigorous images and a great variety of forms and rhythms. An emphasis on the inner life replaces outward description and the old battles with the wilderness. No longer can F. R. Scott complain, as he had in the twenties, about the Miss Crotchet kind of "poetess" going

> From group to chattering group, with such a dear
> Victorian saintliness, as is her fashion,
> Greeting the other unknowns with a cheer —
> Virgins of sixty who still write of passion.

Margaret Avison

For Discussion

1. What aspects of Western Canada are emphasized in recent work by Dorothy Livesay and Miriam Waddington? How does each poet deal with her personal roots in the Prairies? What does the West mean to each poet in retrospect?

2. Love has always been a favourite theme of poets. How love is handled in poetry, however, changes. What kinds of differences do you see between an earlier era's love poetry by Isabella Valancy Crawford and Marjorie Pickthall, and recent love poems by P. K. Page, Miriam Waddington, and Dorothy Livesay?

3. It is not often that an author will write two such contrasting books as Margaret Avison's *Winter Sun* and *The Dumbfounding*. What changes are there in imagery, tone, and rhythm, as well as theme?

For Research

Interview people who lived through the Depression in Canada. How big an impact did it have on their lives? Could they identify with the experiences described in Ann Marriott's *The Wind Our Enemy* and Dorothy Livesay's "The Outrider" and "Day and Night"?

Report on the impact that socialism and communism had on the poems of Dorothy Livesay, Miriam Waddington, and P. K. Page. Which aspects do these poets emphasize? To what effect?

In the poems you have read, what patterns have emerged regarding the ways in which women are portrayed? How would you account for these patterns?

For Reading

Avison, Margaret. *The Dumbfounding*. Norton, 1966.

Avison, Margaret. *Winter Sun*. University of Toronto Press, 1960.

Livesay, Dorothy. *Collected Poems: The Two Seasons*. Ryerson Press, 1972.

Livesay, Dorothy. "Song and Dance." *Canadian Literature*, no. 41 (Summer 1969), 40-48.

Marriott, Anne. *The Wind Our Enemy*. In *The Evolution of Canadian Poetry in English: 1914-1945*, ed. G. L. Parker. Holt, Rinehart & Winston of Canada, 1973.

Page, P. K. *Poems Selected and New*. Anansi, 1974.

Page, P. K. "Questions and Images." *Canadian Literature,* no. 41 (Summer 1969), 17-22.

Waddington, Miriam. *Driving Home: Poems New and Selected*. Oxford University Press of Canada, 1972.

Waddington, Miriam. "Exile: A woman and a stranger living out the Canadian paradox." *Maclean's Magazine,* vol. 87 (March 1974), 40-43.

Jones, L. M. "A Core of Brilliance: Margaret Avison's Achievement." *Canadian Literature,* no. 38 (Autumn 1968), 50-57.

Leland, D. "Dorothy Livesay: Poet of Nature." *Dalhousie Review,* vol. 51 (Autumn 1971), 404-12.

Redekop, E. *Margaret Avison*. Studies in Canadian Literature. Copp Clark, 1970.

Smith, A. J. M. "The Poetry of P. K. Page." *Canadian Literature,* no. 50 (Autumn 1971), 17-27.

Sowton, Ian. "The Lyric Craft of Miriam Waddington." *Dalhousie Review,* vol. 39 (Summer 1959), 237-242.

Stevens, Peter. "Dorothy Livesay: The Love Poetry." *Canadian Literature,* no. 47 (Winter 1971), 26-43.

Wayman, Tom. "Miriam Waddington's New Talent." *Canadian Literature,* no. 56 (Summer 1973), 85-89.

Gabrielle Roy

Chapter 5

Three
French Canadian Writers

French-Canadian and English-Canadian literature have evolved along parallel lines. French-Canadian writers have slowly freed themselves from a post-colonial mentality of looking to France for models, as English-speaking writers have freed themselves from England (and the United States). Victorian moral sensibilities and their effects on the kinds of subject matter published have been mirrored in Quebec by the influence of a strong religious tradition.

The Second World War in effect freed both cultures to go their own ways. After the occupation of France, French publishing houses could no longer be the centres of French-Canadian publication. New presses and companies flourished during the war years in Quebec. When the war was over, France took back the business of editions of the great French continental writers, but French-Canadian publishing carried on. During the war a reading market for French-Canadian work had in fact been created in Quebec.

Gabrielle Roy (born 1909) was one of the first novelists to write for and about twentieth-century Quebec, although she was born in the French-Canadian community of St. Boniface, Manitoba. She was the youngest of eleven children. She was a teacher from 1927 to 1937, first in rural Manitoba and later in St. Boniface; in 1937 she went to Europe to study and write. On her return to Canada in 1939 she decided to stay in Montreal. She worked as a journalist to support herself, while writing in more congenial forms.

She came to know the people in the slum of St. Henri, and wrote a novel to portray their lives, *Bonheur d'occasion* (1945). It was an immediate success. In 1947 it was translated into English as *The Tin Flute*, published in both Toronto and New York, and won the Governor's General's award. It is centred around a large, poor family trying to get by in an industrial and indifferent world. Love, hope and dreams are not enough. There is heavy irony in the fact that war, supplying jobs as soldiers, solves the family's economic problems.

In 1947 Gabrielle Roy was elected to the Royal Society of Canada. Shortly after, she married and moved to France for three years. While she was living there, she won France's prestigious Prix Fémina. In 1950 she returned to Canada and settled in Quebec City. Her second novel, *La petite poule d'eau* (1950; *Where Nests the Water Hen*, 1951) drew on her early teaching experience in northern Manitoba. In it she creates a near-idyll of family solidarity, respect for education (in spite of some unsuitable teachers sent to the remote island), and Christian love.

In *Alexandre Chenevert* (1954; *The Cashier*, 1955), she returned to the sadder streets of Montreal for her setting. The main character is an inconspicuous, unhappy bank teller who seems to have nothing to live for.

Montreal slums, 1946

Standing upright, or with one hip propped against his stool, he felt a great weariness in his back, as though an agonizing pressure on the spinal column forced him to bend over. Yet all his ills were, you might say, his own fault. Thus, at least, had decided the doctor for the insurance company which had issued a policy on his life — occupational maladies, as the doctor had put it.

Gradually, though ill and dying of cancer, he finds closeness to other people and to God. This realistic and compassionate study of the "little man" in urban society was followed by another Manitoba book, *Rue Deschambault* (1955; *Street of Riches,* 1957) . Another Governor General's award winner, it is a series of stories about growing up in Manitoba, loosely based on girlhood memories.

A friend who was a painter, traveller and trapper told her about his trips to the remote North, which became the setting for her next novel, *La montagne secrète* (1961; *The Hidden Mountain,* 1962) . Abandoning her usual character and family study, Gabrielle Roy made this novel a highly symbolic account of the lonely, difficult and dangerous life of the artist. Then she reverted again to her Manitoba experiences in *La route d'Altamont* (1966; *The Road Past Altamont,* 1966) . The four linked stories show the various generation gaps between grandmother, mother and daughter. The basic theme is that no one can truly understand the experiences of someone twenty-five years older until one has oneself experienced those years, and the changes of outlook they bring.

A trip in 1961 to Fort Chimo in Ungava led to three stories and a novel published in 1970 as *La rivière sans repos.* The novel by itself has been translated into English as *Windflower.* All are based on the clash of white and Inuit cultures, and the Inuit as loser. *Windflower* follows the confused and tragic life of Elsa, who in her youth was raped by a white man and bore a son. She raises him alternatively as white and then Inuit, is rejected by him, and returns to the Inuit world as a loner. This bleak story was followed by *Cet été qui chantait* (1972; *Enchanted Summer,* 1976), a much happier collection of nineteen stories about summer life in the cottage country north of Quebec City.

Gabrielle Roy's contribution to the development of the French-Canadian novel has been remarkable, especially in her studies of the urban poor. But the range of her work should be stressed. She writes about the Inuit and immigrants as well as French-Canadians. She writes rural idylls as well as grim city tales. And she has given St. Boniface, a major French-Canadian community outside Quebec, a fictional voice.

Anne Hébert (born 1916) is also concerned with giving French Canada a voice, not a social voice but a much more personal one. Her father was a senior official in Quebec and a literary critic as well. She was an invalid, raised at home and writing from the time she was a child. Long stays in France were a part of her cultural education. Her first book of poetry, *Les songes en équilibre* (1942), somewhat in the symbolist tradition, reveals the subjective life of a sheltered child and young woman, with its dreams and its emotions.

Her second book was a collection of short stories, *Le torrent* (1950; *The Torrent*, 1973), centering on psychological states. *Le tombeau des rois* (1953) was a return to poetry, with imagist impressions of despair, and a solitude verging on claustrophobia:

> There is surely someone
> Killed me
> And slipped off
> On tiptoe
> Missing no beat of his perfected dance.

The haunting soul-searching in some of the poems is circular, and there are no answers.

Anne Hébert

Les chambres de bois (1958; *The Silent Rooms,* 1974), Anne Hébert's first novel, took the Prix France-Canada. The main character, Catherine, escapes from a harsh environment by marrying the son of a rich seigneur. However, her new, more cultured life proves to be unbearable. Her husband pays more attention to his sister than to Catherine, and the unreality of the life they lead in a Paris apartment preys on her. She manages to get away and meets a more vital young man for whom she gives up her suffocating marriage.

In 1960 *Poèmes,* a collected edition of her poetry, was published, and won the Governor General's Award. It contains all of the poems in *Le tombeau des rois,* an essay on the nature of poetry, and sixteen new poems. The newer work is livelier and more positive. Images of bread, water and spring replace the walls and tombs of earlier poems. In 1967 three of her plays appeared in a French edition, and *Le torrent* was reissued with four new stories.

Kamouraska (1970; in English, 1973), her second novel, has been translated into nine languages and made into a major Canadian film. Based loosely on a nineteenth-century murder case, the novel is composed of the imagined thoughts and memories of the woman in the case, Elizabeth d'Aulnières. While outwardly maintaining her role as a model wife in her second marriage, she seethes with old passions.

> They'll never extradite my lover. Charges withdrawn. Two years. Just have to accept things the way they are. Get married again. No veil this time, no orange blossom. Jérôme Rolland, my second husband, and honor is restored. Honor. What an ideal to set yourself when love is what you've lost.

We gradually piece together the story of her early first marriage to an insane and brutal man, her separation from him and affair with an American doctor, and the murder of the husband. Elizabeth's strong emotions were subsequently reined in by nineteenth-century pressures to be a "lady," but her memories could not be checked.

Kamouraska, 1784

In both the novels and the poetry, Anne Hébert has concentrated on the inner life of the individual, usually a woman, caged in by tradition or by other people. Her protagonists need emotional fulfilment. This is equally true of her third novel, *Les enfants du sabbat* (1975; *Children of the Black Sabbath,* 1977), which takes in the demonic as well.

Marie-Claire Blais (born 1939) is Canada's best-known French-Canadian novelist, with fourteen novels to her credit as well as poems, plays, and prose-poems. Born in a Quebec City slum and raised in a convent school, she left at fifteen to earn money. She had started to write at the age of nine, and her preoccupation with her writing made her a less than perfect employee in a series of small jobs. She was rescued from the usual fate of the urban poor by a university dean who saw her manuscript of *La belle bête*. He was impressed by her able and powerful prose, and helped to get the novel published in 1959, when she was twenty. It was immediately translated into English as *Mad Shadows* (1960), and has since been made into a ballet.

Mad Shadows is the unrelievedly bleak and unhappy story of twisted relationships among the members of a family on a rural estate. The narcissistic mother reserves her love for her handsome idiot son, and the ugly but clever daughter is passionately jealous. Disfigurement and murder are the results of various hatreds, and the family house is destroyed.

Her second novel, *Tête Blanche* (1960; in English, 1961) is no happier. The setting is urban and the social class of the family described high enough to have a son sent to private school. The focus is on this son, mainly ignored by his actress-mother. He becomes alienated, proud, and attracted to evil. The effect of the death of his mother is somewhat lightened by his first adolescent love, but then the girl disappears. His old tutor also abandons him, in a sense, to the process of growing up. Loveless and feeling betrayed, he ends by writing his own philosophy of life:

> All I have is the strength to hate, the strength of pride; the other, the strength and the patience for love, I no longer have.
> Life is a lie.

Marie-Claire Blais then turned to poetry (two volumes appeared in French) and novellas written in what might be called prose poetry. Her work was hailed by Edmund Wilson of *The New Yorker,* then engaged in a study of Canadian history and literature later published as *O Canada.* He helped her get a Guggenheim fellowship. She spent a year in Paris, and then for seven years lived on Cape Cod in Massachusetts, well away from her roots in Quebec City. She isolated herself in order to write.

Un saison dans la vie d'Emmanuel (1965; *A Season in the Life of Emmanuel,* 1966) is set in a small town surrounded by farmland. It is the story of a very poor French Canadian family, told initially from the point of view of the sixteenth baby on the day of his birth:

> Born without fuss, this winter morning, Emmanuel was listening to his grandmother's voice. Immense and all-powerful, she seemed to be ruling the whole world from her armchair. (Don't cry, what have you got to cry about? Your mother has gone back to work on the farm. Just you keep quiet until she gets home...)

This novel presents life as a survival test. The dominating grandmother and the brutal father, at odds with each other, both have the resources for survival. No one else seems safe; already half the children are dead. The misery of the children and their various attempts to get away provide most of the action. The novel was awarded France's Prix Médicis.

In her next novels Marie-Claire Blais concentrated on the emotional life of adolescence. *L'insoumise* (1966), explores psychological reactions to the death of a teenage boy in those who knew him. In *David Sterne* (1967), the teenage characters investigate and consciously choose lives of vice, leading to death. The black mood of these novels is somewhat relieved by the work which followed. The first, *Manuscrits de Pauline Archange* (1968), won the Governor General's award. It was followed by *Vivre! Vivre!* (1969) and *Les apparences* (1970). The first two have been translated together as *The Manuscripts of Pauline Archange* (1970).

For the first time, in this semi-autobiographical series, the main character is a girl. Pauline's childhood is spent looking at her home and the neighbourhood with fearless eyes. Regularly branded as a heartless monster, she snatches what rebellious joys she can in the atmosphere of guilt and shame created for children by parents and nuns. Her main escape is her writing, as it had been for one of the dying children in *A Season in the Life of Emmanuel.* There is more hope in the *Manuscripts:* Pauline is no archangel but she will definitely survive.

Marie-Claire Blais moved in the early seventies to a small community in Brittany, France, and wrote there for four years. *Le loup* (1972; *The Wolf,* 1974) is a study of dangerous and violent emotions among homosexual boys and men. Then in *Un joualonais, sa joualonerie* (1973; *St. Lawrence Blues,* 1974) she returned to urban low life, this time in Montreal, in a new

Marie-Claire Blais

Mlle Blais is a true "phenomenon;" she may possibly be a genius. At the age of twenty-four, she has produced four remarkable books of a passionate and poetic force that, as far as my reading goes, is not otherwise to be found in French Canadian fiction.

Edmund Wilson, in O Canada *(Farrar, Straus & Giroux, 1965)*

Women in rural Quebec were still using outdoor ovens like this one, at Cap à l'Aigle, well into the twentieth century.

satiric vein. The French title indicates the concern with "joual," the French dialect that has been recently championed as the proper language for dialogue in Québécois literature instead of Parisian French. There is a good deal more sympathy for the down-and-out inhabitants of the underworld and its fringes than for the middle-class poet who sets out to learn "joual" and write it:

> "I wrote a little masterpiece in Joualonese; it was so pure it almost stank. I thought, my compatriots will recognize themselves in this. I'd spoken like the man in the street, the woman of the sidewalks, the child on his scooter, dispelling the symbolic and rural shadow of Maria Chapdelaine. What happens? Once again I was bitterly attacked, *mon cher,* the critics said I didn't understand the Joualonese soul . . ."

Various Marxist and humanist theorizers about the problems of the poor also come in for attack.

Marie-Claire Blais has returned to the province of Quebec and is living and writing there after twelve years abroad. Her work has a vast range, from poetic interior monologue to realistic external description, from lyric to satiric. She is at home in both urban and rural settings, upper class and lower class. She has freed French-Canadian literature from less than frank treatments of "la belle province." An older literary tradition of glorifying the past, the family, and religious life has been turned upside down. She has chosen to expose the black misery, financial or emotional, that can exist in people's lives today, and does so with savage intensity.

1. Love, marriage, and the family circle are of prime interest in many novels, including French-Canadian ones. Compare the treatment of these themes, and the particular roles of women, in a much earlier novel about Quebec, Louis Hémon's *Maria Chapdelaine*, and Anne Hébert's *Kamouraska*.

2. Life in the slums is more than mere setting in Gabrielle Roy's *The Tin Flute* and Marie-Claire Blais' *Manuscripts of Pauline Archange*. It is a dominating force. How is it presented in these two novels? What differences are there in the characters' responses to economic hardship and poor living conditions?

3. The dominating female character is a recurring figure in French-Canadian literature. How similar are Grandmère Antoinette in *A Season in the Life of Emmanuel* and Luzina in *Where Nests the Water Hen*? Does the fact that Luzina lives in isolated northern Manitoba make much difference?

Investigate and report on earlier developments in French-Canadian literature. In how many ways does its evolution parallel that of English-Canadian literature? What differences do you find? What reasons can you find to explain these differences?

Marie-Claire Blais has often concentrated on the mental and emotional lives of children and adolescents. Do you find Lucie in *Mad Shadows* and the title character of *Tête Blanche* credible? What aspects of teenage life have been emphasized? To what effect?

Jean-le-Maigre in *A Season in the Life of Emmanuel* and Pauline in *Manuscripts of Pauline Archange* can temporarily escape their environment by writing about it. Choose one aspect of your personal environment and write about it. Evaluate the experience gained from putting your thoughts on paper. Consider your experience in the light of those of Jean-le-Maigre and Pauline. Is it possible to truly escape one's environment by writing about it, or do you feel that writing is really a way of learning to cope with reality? Discuss.

For Reading

Blais, Marie-Claire. *The Manuscripts of Pauline Archange*. Bantam, 1976.

Blais, Marie-Claire. *Mad Shadows*. New Canadian Library #78. McClelland & Stewart, 1971.

Blais, Marie-Claire. *A Season in the Life of Emmanuel*. Bantam, 1976.

Blais, Marie-Claire. *Tête Blanche*. New Canadian Library #104. McClelland & Stewart, 1974.

Hébert, Anne. *Kamouraska*. Paperjacks. General Publishing, 1974.

Hébert, Anne. *Poems by Anne Hébert,* trans. Alan Brown. Musson, 1975.

Hébert, Anne. *The Silent Rooms*. Paperjacks. General Publishing, 1975.

Roy, Gabrielle. *The Cashier*. New Canadian Library #40. McClelland & Stewart, 1963.

Roy, Gabrielle. *The Tin Flute*. New Canadian Library #5. Toronto, McClelland & Stewart, 1958.

Roy, Gabrielle. *Where Nests the Water Hen*. New Canadian Library #25. McClelland & Stewart, 1961.

Grosskurth, Phyllis. *Gabrielle Roy*. Canadian Writers Series. Toronto: Forum, 1969.

Hind-Smith, Joan. *Three Voices: The Lives of Margaret Laurence, Gabrielle Roy, Frederick Philip Grove*. Clarke Irwin, 1975.

Macri, F. M. "Anne Hébert: Story and Poem." *Canadian Literature,* no. 58 (Autumn 1973), 9-18.

Mezei, Kathy. "Anne Hébert: A Pattern Repeated." *Canadian Literature,* no. 72 (Spring 1977), 29-40.

McPherson, Hugo. "The Garden and the Cage: The Achievement of Gabrielle Roy." *Canadian Literature,* no. 1 (Summer 1959), 46-57.

Russell, George. "Nightmare's Child: Marie-Claire Blais has brought her chilling universe back to Quebec." *Weekend Magazine,* October 23, 1976, 11-13.

Stratford, Philip. *Marie-Claire Blais*. Canadian Writers Series. Toronto: Forum, 1970.

Developments in Fiction

Since the Second World War, the novel in Canada has been dramatically wider in scope. It may be a traditional moral tale, or may look at moral issues without comment as in the work of Marie-Claire Blais. It may have a local, regional, national, or international setting. It may stress individual identity or much wider social interests.

Ethel Wilson (born 1890) writes a good old-fashioned novel with a happy ending. Raised in South Africa, Canada, and England, she made Vancouver her home and taught school there until her marriage in 1930. She began her literary career with short stories during the thirties, but came to Canadian notice properly with the publication of *Hetty Dorval*, her first novel, in 1947. It was followed fairly rapidly by *The Innocent Traveller* (1949) , *The Equations of Love* (1952) , *Swamp Angel* (1954) and *Love and Salt Water* (1956) . A collection of her short stories appeared in 1961 as *Mrs. Golightly and Other Stories*.

Hetty Dorval deals with innocence and experience. A young Canadian girl, Frankie, comes into contact with the beautiful, charming, but totally unscrupulous adventuress, Hetty. Gradually Frankie finds out the truth, becomes a rival to Hetty in a man's affections, and the novel ends with the exposure of Hetty. Though the setting is international in scope, the book is remarkable for its descriptions of British Columbia. Hetty's only good point, one she shares with Frankie, is a love for the land.

Ethel Wilson

Title pages of a special edition of Hetty Dorval, *printed in 1967*

HETTY
DORVÁL

by Ethel Wilson

1967
THE ALCUIN SOCIETY
VANCOUVER, BRITISH COLUMBIA

The Innocent Traveller is a series of stories about the British in Vancouver, and is gently satiric about the English who remain English no matter how long they live in a new environment. *Equations of Love* contains two stories. "Tuesday and Wednesday" is set among lower class people who have makeshift lives and impossible dreams. "Lilly's Story" returns to the tradition of the happy ending; an orphan girl grows up and in spite of poor environment makes a new life for herself and her illegitimate daughter.

Swamp Angel, Ethel Wilson's most famous novel, has two major female characters, neither involved in the usual love story. One is Maggie Vardoe, who carefully plans her escape from an impossible husband and goes to work as a cook in a fishing lodge in British Columbia. The other is Mrs. Severance, an old, fat circus performer who is both comic and wise without being an angel. Nature plays a healing role for Maggie, but the author allows that there are some people who are not wilderness enthusiasts:

> "I don't care for fresh air myself except for the purpose of breathing. I exist here . . . and here . . ." Mrs. Severance touched her heart and her head. "Everything of any importance happens indoors . . ."
>
> "Oh, it does not!" said Maggie.
>
> ". . . including eating and sleeping."

Various problems in human relationships surface for both of them and are gradually resolved through love and friendship. While in no way figures that would now be called "liberated women," both Maggie and Mrs. Severance are strong characters who function well on their own.

In *Love and Salt Water*, Ethel Wilson's passion for nature moves her to choose a high seas setting for a romantic story. A girl engaged to be married has her facial beauty destroyed when she rescues her nephew in a boating accident. The question of her fiancé's devotion is easily resolved, and the happy ending follows. The novel's high points, though, are the descriptions of the sea: the voyage to England, a storm at sea, and a riptide.

The novels of Ethel Wilson tend to reward good (and love) and punish evil. However, they are far from syrupy. An element of wit and humour recurs to lighten the predicament of the characters. Her perception into the lives of unusual people, the Hetty Dorvals, the Maggie Vardoes, and the Mrs. Severances of the world, gives these characters a distinct vitality of their own. Equally alive is her treatment of nature, particularly the wilderness.

New ground in Canadian fiction was broken with the publication of Sheila Watson's *The Double Hook*, which moves far beyond the usual realistic or romantic conventions. Sheila Watson (born 1919) was born in British Columbia and educated there and in Toronto. She is married to the poet Wilfred Watson and they both teach at the University of Alberta. She is an

Sheila Watson

authority on the works of the British artist and writer, Wyndham Lewis, and is working on his biography. As a writer she has published a few short stories but is widely known for *The Double Hook*, a short novel quite unlike anything else in our literature.

The Double Hook concerns a very isolated community in the Rockies and its inhabitants. Some of the incidents could have been written in a melodramatic style — there is murder, a blinding, an illegitimate birth, madness and arson. However, these elements are raised to the level of symbolic, almost allegorical, action. The community wavers between negatives (drought, death, the howling of the coyote) and positives (new crops, a baby, renewed spiritual communal life) . Allusions to Christianity and to both Amerindian and European myths enrich the spare style. Greta, the daughter of the murdered woman, goes mad and burns down the family house around her, following the self-destructive pattern of the negative forces:

> The words of the lord came, saying: Say now to the rebellious house, Know you not what these things mean?
>
> Greta had inherited destruction like a section surveyed and fenced. She had lived no longer than the old lady's shadow left its stain on the ground. She sat in her mother's doom as she sat in her chair.

The novel ends with a muted affirmation of the life forces, physical and spiritual.

The title refers to Sheila Watson's motto, that life is a search with a double catch, that "when you fish for the glory you catch the darkness too." In direct opposition to the tradition of regional novels and rural idylls, *The Double Hook* has universal themes and its setting could be anywhere. It is a creative expression of the twentieth century's interest in archetypes and myths.

Scenes from the Winnipeg Jewish community in the 1920s

Adele Wiseman

Adele Wiseman, on the other hand, has written two novels notable for their specifically urban and ethnic themes. Born in Winnipeg in 1928, she has had a varied career, teaching in Italy, being an editor in England, teaching at McGill's Macdonald College, and being executive secretary for the Royal Wninipeg Ballet. Her first novel, *The Sacrifice* (1956) draws on the background that she and Miriam Waddington share, that of the East European Jewish immigrants to Western Canada.

The Sacrifice centres around Abraham, the butcher, and his family. Two sons are already dead, sacrificed in a pogrom in the old land. A third son tries to live up to his father's expectations and dies of a heart attack. Abraham, who had wanted to be a rabbi and still feels that God has a special interest in him, cannot face his responsibility for this death.

> How had his dream appeared to them, his sons? Had they seen him as Ruth saw him, as he now saw himself? Was it for his own pride that he had dreamed his sons into heroes, so that he could boast that he was the father of such marvels?

He goes mad, ritually murders a woman, and finishes in a psychiatric hospital. The novel ends with a more hopeful outlook for the grandson, Moses, who becomes reconciled to Abraham the murderer.

The same Winnipeg and Jewish background is used to more comic effect in Adele Wiseman's second novel, *Crackpot* (1974). The title character is Hoda, the fat, loving, quick-tempered neighbourhood prostitute. As a motherless teenager she sets out to work for herself and her blind father. She gradually descends to prostitution when she finds it easier than being a charwoman. Through tragedy and comedy she manages, and cares for her father. At the end of the novel a lonely survivor of European anti-semitism doggedly woos her, and Hoda decides to finally marry.

Both *The Sacrifice* and *Crackpot* are rich in characters of all ages. Adele Wiseman has a gift for creating larger-than-life, memorable and interesting characters such as Abraham and Hoda. In their very different ways they are both on the side of life, the family, the future. She has also written out of her own memories about one of the centres of immigrant life, the local market. *Old Markets, New World* (1964) combines her reminiscences with Joe Rosenthal's drawings.

The work of Alice Munro (born 1931) goes back to the world of the small town. She was raised in a southwestern Ontario town which becomes her fictional "Jubilee," in spite of the fact that she has spent most of her adult life in British Columbia where she and her first husband ran a bookstore. She is something of a specialist in short story writing, and her work often appears in *The Tamarack Review, The Canadian Forum,* and *Chatelaine,* and is read over the CBC.

Her first book-length collection appeared as *Dance of the Happy Shades* in 1968. These stories are usually narrated by girls or young women trying to cope with the pressure of growing up, being jilted, or facing illness and death in the family. Alice Munro has concentrated on evoking the psychological realities of small-town life. For instance, in the title story it is clear that the town mothers will never again accept the old music teacher's invitations, because the best player at the annual recital is a retarded child and not one of their own.

Lives of Girls and Women (1971) is subtitled "A Novel" but is more a series of eight related stories, episodes in the childhood and adolescence of Del Jordan. She is a sensitive and inquiring character, set apart from the inhabitants of Jubilee in two ways: she is bright enough to hope for scholarships and escape, and her mother is an eccentric encyclopedia saleswoman. Her best friend Naomi shares the typical lot of the small-town girl, leaving school early, getting pregnant, and getting married for convenience's sake. Although Del finally manages to have an affair, she is spared Naomi's fate and resolves to escape and be a writer. She later reflects:

> People's lives, in Jubilee as elsewhere, were dull, simple, amazing and unfathomable — deep caves lined with kitchen linoleum.
> It did not occur to me then that one day I would be so greedy for Jubilee. Voracious and misguided as Uncle Craig out at Jenkin's Bend, writing his History, I would want to write things down.

Alice Munro's next work, *Something I've been Meaning to Tell You* (1974) is a collection of twelve stories, some set in southern Ontario and some in British Columbia. The main characters are again women, this time older, trying to cope with

Alice Munro

A subject race has a kind of clarity of vision and I feel that women have always had a clarity of vision which men were denied. . . . In a way, our clear-sightedness stems from our not having power.

Alice Munro, in Chatelaine, *August, 1975*

the positions they find themselves in, both emotionally and socially. In her best work, Alice Munro is very perceptive about the way women react to men and to the conditioning of their early lives which prepares them more for a "battle of the sexes" than anything else. She is now remarried and again living in southwestern Ontario.

Marian Engel (born 1933) covers the same ground but also reaches out to a wider world both geographically and socially. Raised in five Ontario towns and cities, she first committed herself to an academic life. She studied, tutored and taught in Montreal, England, France and Cyprus. In 1962 she married. In 1964 she returned to Toronto for a life as a wife, the mother of twins, and a serious writer. The basic material of her novels is the lives of women she has observed, raised in the forties and fifties like herself and not really prepared for all the facts of life, nor for women's liberation.

Her first novel, *No Clouds of Glory* (1968; in paperback, *Sarah Bastard's Notebook*) is about a single, supposedly independent, respected teacher of English literature. Under the surface, Sarah is unhappy, alienated from her family, and trying to get over an affair with her Italian brother-in-law and the ensuing abortion. Her various guilt feelings are well portrayed. Her small rebellions, in beer and four-letter words, do not solve her problems. The novel ends with her decision to chuck it all, sell her possessions, and move to Montreal in hopes of finding something better.

The heroine of *The Honeyman Festival* (1970), on the other hand, is married and pregnant with her fourth child. The novel is an account of the events and rambling thoughts of one night in the life of Minn Burge. There is considerable humour in it, satire on the film industry, and a finale in which Minn assaults a policeman for overstepping the bounds of authority. The old, untidy house, the coffee, cigarettes and liquor, the dishes and the diapers, her life as it really is in downtown Toronto is analyzed and finally accepted by Minn. She rejects the manuals and the magazines that set impossible goals, "the perfect housekeeper, the perfect disciplinarian, the perfect mother." She can cope, even with the guilt feelings these goals give her.

In *Monodromos* (1973; in paperback, *One-Way Street*) Marian Engel returns to some of the problems of *No Clouds of Glory*. Audrey Moore goes to Cyprus in response to a distress telegram from her ex-husband, a homosexual musician. But, as it turns out, he did not send it, and does not want her. She stays anyway for the sunshine and the warmth of the people she meets, but something is always lacking.

> There has to be more to that big abstraction we call life for want of a better word than food on a plate, cash in the till, legs in a bed, there is more, the people here know it. But I don't know what it is. I'm one of those opaque lady travellers after all, who sees, but does not understand.

Marian Engel

The odd comic touch, about the streets and ways of Cyprus, does little to relieve Audrey's problems as a Canadian abroad in worlds she does not understand.

A village in Cyprus

In 1973 Marian Engel was elected the first chairman of The Writers' Union of Canada. She was frequently a contributor to magazines at this time, with articles and book reviews. In 1975 a collection of her short stories, *Inside the Easter Egg*, was published. Then she wrote *Bear*, which explores one of her favourite themes — women's problems in coming to terms with sexuality — in a different way.

Bear (1976), which took the Governor General's Award in 1977, does not have Marian Engel's usual urban setting and lower or middle-class milieu. Lou, an archivist, is sent north to an island estate to catalogue documents left by an eccentric colonel. Quite a few of the documents record myths and facts about bears, and an old tame bear is her only companion. The short novel develops her growing love for the bear, erotic as well as companionable, in an understated and believable way.

The Writers' Union provides a forum for communication among writers, between writers and publishers, and between writers and the public. It also provides services in the area of contracts, copyrights, and other professional matters.

The bear eventually claws Lou. When she recovers, she feels renewed. She is proud of the fact that she has been able to live on her own terms. Her retreat to the wilderness is temporary; the job is done, the bear will hibernate, she is really a stranger and must return to the city. She leaves the island, apparently to find a new job and a new life. For once, there is a very positive tone at the end of the novel, and the Canadian wilderness is no longer the enemy.

Modern fiction written by women has often focussed on women as main characters, though *The Double Hook* and *The Sacrifice* show that this is not always the case. Open discussion of women's liberation, of sexuality and of economic and social choice have been reflected in the fiction, sometimes directly, but more often indirectly. However, these novels and short stories should not, by any means, be characterized as "women's" literature. The entire society, not just that of women, is always there. The recurring themes which characterize Canadian literature, such as identity problems, the search for values, and relationships with nature, are given new expression.

In the last generation, Canadian fiction has finally grown up. The day of the sentimental and moral tale, with its closed ending, seems to be over. The realistic, open-ended novel, more concerned with individual problems than with love duets is here to stay.

For Discussion

1. Immigrant life in Winnipeg is the focus for Laura Goodman Salverson's *Confessions of an Immigrant's Daughter* and, more recently, Adele Wiseman's *The Sacrifice*. Have things changed much for the first-generation immigrant man or woman?

2. Adolescence involves a number of adjustment processes, some more difficult than others. What are the trials and tribulations of the adolescent Frankie in Ethel Wilson's *Hetty Dorval* and Del in Alice Munro's *Lives of Girls and Women*? Can you identify with their experiences? If so, in what ways? What effect does the fact that they live in small communities have on their growing up? In your opinion, would a city setting significantly affect the adolescent's responses in these novels? Why?

Evaluate the strength of the "back to nature" movement in your community. Interview men and women who have lived, even if temporarily, in the wilderness. How has it affected them? What similarities or differences are there in their reactions? Compare their reactions to those of Maggie, in Ethel Wilson's *Swamp Angel,* or Lou, in Marian Engel's *Bear.*

If you have studied Amerindian and/or classical European mythology, discuss the parallels to the characters and situations in Sheila Watson's *The Double Hook*. What do they add to your reading of the novel?

For Research

For Reading

Engel, Marian. *Bear*. McClelland & Stewart, 1976.

Engel, Marian. *The Honeyman Festival*. Anansi, 1970.

Munro, Alice. *Lives of Girls and Women*. McGraw-Hill Ryerson, 1971. Also in paperback: New American Library, 1974.

Munro, Alice. *Something I've Been Meaning to Tell You*. McGraw-Hill Ryerson, 1974. Also in paperback: New American Library, 1975.

Watson, Sheila. *The Double Hook*. New Canadian Library #54. McClelland & Stewart, 1966.

Wilson, Ethel. *Hetty Dorval*. Laurentian Library #6. Macmillan of Canada, 1967.

Wilson, Ethel. *Swamp Angel*. New Canadian Library #29. McClelland & Stewart, 1962.

Wiseman, Adele. *The Sacrifice*. Laurentian Library #8. Macmillan of Canada, 1968.

Wiseman, Adele. *Crackpot*. McClelland & Stewart, 1974.

Birbalsingh, Frank. "Ethel Wilson: Innocent Traveller." *Canadian Literature,* no. 49 (Summer 1971), 35-46.

Gibson, Graeme. Interview with Marian Engel, in his *Eleven Canadian Novelists*. Anansi, 1973.

Monkman, Leslie. "Coyote as Trickster in *The Double Hook*." *Canadian Literature,* no. 52 (Spring 1972), 70-76.

Mullins, Stanley E. "Traditional Symbolism in Adele Wiseman's *The Sacrifice*." *Culture,* vol. 19 (September 1958), 287-297.

Murch, Ken. "Name: Alice Munro, Occupation: Writer." *Chatelaine,* vol. 48 (August 1975), 42-43, 69-72.

Polk, James. "Deep Caves and Kitchen Linoleum." *Canadian Literature,* no. 54 (Autumn 1972), 102-104. (Alice Munro).

Pacey, Desmond. *Ethel Wilson*. Twayne's World Authors. Boston: Twayne, 1968.

Chapter 7

Aspects of Contemporary Poetry

After 1939 the left-wing cause lost some of its hold on poets. During the forties, lively debates in Canada about the nature of poetry — "original" or "aboriginal", intellectual or visceral, realistic or symbolic, objective or subjective or mythic — released a lot of creative energy. As a result, Canadian poetry is said by many to have really "arrived" during the fifties and sixties. There was increasing publication of poetry by both the traditional companies and new small presses. Established poets like Dorothy Livesay and Miriam Waddington moved both into new areas of subject matter and into professional criticism. Among the increasing number of women coming to national notice are Elizabeth Brewster, Phyllis Gotlieb, Jay Macpherson and Gwendolyn MacEwen.

Elizabeth Brewster (born 1922) is a national figure in more ways than one: she has lived in most parts of Canada. Born and raised in New Brunswick, she has studied there, in Massachusetts (at Radcliffe), in Toronto, in England, and in Indiana. She has worked mainly as a librarian (teaching creative writing at times) in New Brunswick, Ontario, British Columbia and Alberta. She is at the time of this writing a member of the English Department at the University of Saskatchewan.

Her poems first appeared in little magazines, and then in three booklets, *East Coast* (1951), *Lillooet* (1954), and *Roads and Other Poems* (1957). She was one of *Five New Brunswick Poets* (1962). Many of these early poems were included in her first major book, *Passages of Summer* (1969). The tone is often nostalgic as she looks back on her New Brunswick upbringing, her family and neighbours, and a typical village (a West Coast one this time) lovingly described in "Lillooet." Easily accessible on first reading, there are poems of all kinds — narratives, imagist work like "Orange Rooster," sonnets, songs and elegies. They record the thoughts of a sharp but charitable observer, mocking the so-called progress of modern civilization. In "Atlantic Development," for instance, she sees

> Three abandoned churches in a row;
> Tombstones behind them hidden by waving timothy . . .
> In the neighbouring village
> The only young men on the street are these granite soldiers
> Carved on the war memorial in front of the Post Office.

Elizabeth Brewster's ironic sense also shows up in a series of portraits of farming people and small-town types.

Sunrise North (1972) is different from earlier work, although it contains poems about New Brunswick and family matters. Many of the poems describe Alberta, more northern, colder and hotter by turns than her previous homes. A number of the poems are more subjective, especially a series of love poems. This trend is continued in *In Search of Eros* (1974), a volume that shows a good deal of interest in old mythologies, nursery tales, and characters from literature. The title poem retells the story of Psyche, losing and then searching for her love, Eros. There are

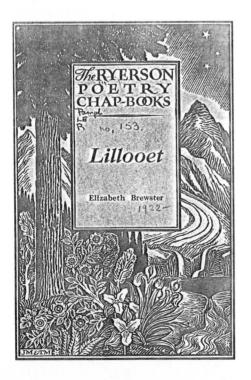

Cover from Lillooet *in the Ryerson Chap-Book series*

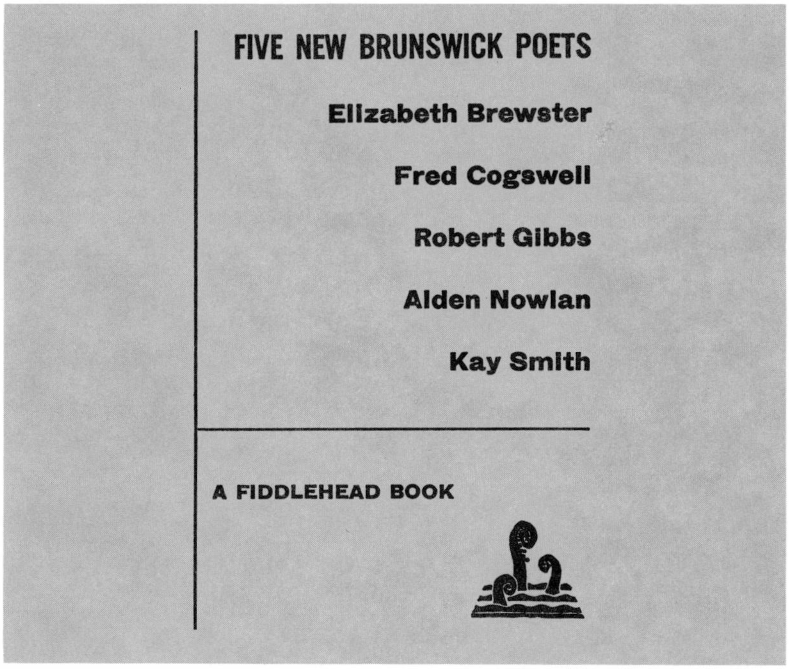

FIVE NEW BRUNSWICK POETS

Elizabeth Brewster

Fred Cogswell

Robert Gibbs

Alden Nowlan

Kay Smith

A FIDDLEHEAD BOOK

Cover from a limited edition of
Five New Brunswick Poets

also personal love lyrics, and comments about the world of poets. She ironically dismisses herself from the status of established poet because she is ladylike and can spell and punctuate properly.

Elizabeth Brewster's poetry is notable for its sensitive rendering of various emotions and landscapes. At times she is a humanist, at other times a detached observer of small moments and details. She has also written a novel, *The Sisters* (1974), about growing up in rural New Brunswick. Her next work was another volume of poetry, *Sometimes I Think Of Moving* (1977).

Phyllis Gotlieb (born 1926) is a woman of various literary talents. Born and raised in Toronto, and educated at the University of Toronto, she uses her third-generation East-European Jewish background in two aspects of her work, her poetry and her Canadian novel. Cultural heritage, street life and her observations as wife and mother are reflected in her booklet *Who Knows One* (1961) and her two collections of poems, *Within the Zodiac* (1964) and *Ordinary, Moving* (1969). In the latter volume especially, children's rhymes, old phone numbers, new versions of old Negro spirituals, Jewish prayers, love poems and graffiti are mixed with references to Catullus, Villon and Byron in a potpourri that is lively and almost mischievous.

The long closing poem, "Ordinary, Moving," is a magnificent work about childhood in all moods and cultures, happy and nightmarish:

> under my bed, my childhood bed
> only the dustflocks blew
> in the midnight caverns of my head
> the goblins spawned and grew

Phyllis Gotlieb's language and imagery are often those of the street — cement, dandelions, bridge spans, subways and movie theatres all come under scrutiny.

Her Canadian novel, *Why Should I Have All the Grief?* (1969) also uses a Jewish background, though not her own. The main character, Heinz Dorfman, is a survivor of the most infamous of the German concentration camps, Auschwitz, and lives in Toronto. The novel probes the question of guilt in those who survived:

> *I have suffered; suffering is punishment; therefore, because I have been punished, I must have been judged guilty of something.* It was a flawed syllogism of the human spirit.

In the three days spent in mourning for an unloved relative, he finally comes to grips with his past, especially his hatred of his father, who is portrayed as a powerful, miserly villain.

Phyllis Gotlieb has also been associated with the CBC. It has commissioned a number of radio dramas from her, such as "Dr. Umlaut's Earthly Kingdom." In addition, she is well known in the United States as a science fiction writer. Her stories appear in such American magazines as *Amazing, Galaxy* and *Fantasy.* Two of her science fiction novels have been published in New York: *Sunburst* (1964) and *O Master Caliban* (1976). In Canada her reputation rests mainly on her poetry, for her reworking of the world of children and the Jewish heritage, and a rare sense of fun.

Phyllis Gotlieb

The poetry of Jay Macpherson (born 1931) is very different from Elizabeth Brewster's rural descriptions and Phyllis Gotlieb's Toronto street songs. Born in England, Jay Macpherson came to Canada as a child. Her university education took her to Ottawa, England, Montreal and Toronto. An academic all her adult life, she teaches English Literature at Victoria College in the University of Toronto at the time of this writing.

Her poetry reflects her teaching career. She is steeped in the Bible and classical mythology and the entire range of English literature. She has been influenced by the mythopoeic view of poetry, which sees all imaginative writing throughout history as re-creations of a few, universal, deeply-rooted patterns or archetypes — primarily the life cycle in man and nature.

Two early booklets, *Nineteen Poems* (1952) and *O Earth Return* (1954) set the high standards in craftsmanship that are seen in all of her work. The first was published at Robert Graves' press on the island of Majorca; Robert Graves is one of the leading international proponents of the mythopoeic school. Jay Macpherson's skill in mythmaking was recognized in 1957 when her first major book, *The Boatman,* won the Governor General's award. As one of its six sequences it includes the earlier "O Earth Return." Psyche, the Phoenix, The Abominable Snowman, Cain and Abel and Noah are all re-created in short poems with traditional structures and rhymes.

> The world was first a private park
> Until the angel, after dark,
> Scattered afar to wests and easts
> The lovers and the friendly beasts.

This volume was re-issued in 1968 with sixteen new poems as *The Boatman and Other Poems.*

In 1975 she privately printed *Welcoming Disaster: Poems 1970-1974.* In a serio-comic way she reworks classical mythological descents into the underworld. Humour is provided by the irony of the narrator and the presence of the teddy-bear she had as a child. The titles of the sequences indicate the structure of the journey: "Invocations", "The Way Down", "Recognitions", and "Shadows Flee." The cycle ends with the falling apart of the old toy, and the ghosts and goblins are laid to rest.

Jay Macpherson's use of literary echoes and her concentration on the major patterns of myth make her work less accessible to the general reader. On the other hand, her simple vocabulary and her use of regular song-like stanzas can be readily grasped, as can her sense of irony and wit. In keeping with her main interests, she has written for young readers *The Four Ages of Man* (1962), a prose account of classical mythology.

Gwendolyn MacEwen is another prominent member of the mythopoeic school. Born in Toronto in 1941, she left school at eighteen in order to write, and was then married briefly to the poet Milton Acorn. At the age of twenty she had her early work printed in two booklets, *The Drunken Clock* and *Selah.* After a

[Jay Macpherson] is the first Canadian poet to carve angels at all well. No one before had ever told Canadian poets that the Angel was or could be a very suitable and good topic for poetry.

from James Reaney, "The Third Eye," *in George Woodcock, ed.,* A Choice of Critics *(Oxford University Press, 1966)*

Cover from a hand-printed presentation copy of O Earth Return

visit to Israel, she produced her first novel, *Julian the Magician,* and a major book of poems, *The Rising Fire*, in 1963. *Julian the Magician* is an unusual novel set in an older, superstitious European country. The title character is a wandering magician trained in alchemy and mystical writings. He comes to see parallels between his magic and Christ's miracles. The parallels build until he too loses his life, much as Christ did.

Gwendolyn MacEwen's early poems use Greek, Christian and Babylonian myth, often in juxtaposition with contemporary images, to work out patterns in our experience and make sense of the fragmented modern world. Original chaos was at least whole:

> A woman called Chaos, she
> was the earth inebriate, without form,
> a thing of ripped green flesh
> and forests in crooked wooden dance
> and water a wine drunk on itself
> and boulders bumping into foolish clouds.

A Breakfast for Barbarians (1966) and *The Shadow-Maker* (1969), which won the Governor General's award, take this

Gwendolen MacEwen

interest in myths and relate the archetypal patterns to her own personal thoughts and experiences.

A Breakfast for Barbarians contains a prose introduction in which the poet outlines her intentions. She offers her breakfast menu of poems to be absorbed by her readers:

> The particular horrors of the present civilization have been painted starkly enough. The key theme of things is the alienation, the exile from our own inventions, and hence from ourselves. Let's say No — rather enclose, absorb, and have done. The intake.

Perhaps this helps to explain why her landscapes are likely to be from the less technological Middle East, if anywhere. The poems in the volume are full of life. *The Shadow-Maker* is a contrasting volume. In its four sections, "Holy Terrors", 'The Unspeakable", "The Sleeper" and "The Shadow-Maker", it tries to come to grips with evil, darkness, and psychological demons. Even love has an ambiguous air about it.

Ancient mythological dramas are recreated for modern audiences in a Greek amphitheatre.

From the tomb of Ramses II, Abu Simbel.

A Canada Council grant enabled Gwendolyn MacEwen to go to Egypt in 1966 to study the background for her second novel, *King of Egypt, King of Dreams* (1971) . This historical novel is her interpretation of the life and reign of Akhenaton, the Egyptian ruler who tried to change the official religion of Egypt to monotheism over three thousand years ago. She re-creates Akhenaton's unsuccessful efforts to communicate the mystery of his sun-worship, and his neglect of the political arena.

A trip to Greece in 1971 and her marriage to a Greek singer are reflected in her next volume of poems, *Armies of the Moon* (1972) . Ancient Greece is not forgotten, as "A Letter to Charos" shows. Quite a number of these poems are written in a personal voice, though the poet adopts a number of modern *personae* such as the airplane captain and the president of the Flat Earth Society. The opening and closing poems are written in the light of an event which must have delighted Gwendolyn MacEwen — the astronauts' landing on the myth-laden moon. In 1972 she also brought together her short stories in *Noman*, a collection dealing with strong psychological forces.

In 1974 she selected poems from all of her previous work and added twenty-eight more to make up *Magic Animals*. The poetry is still that of oracles, gods, souls, and centaurs.

> What dove gone mad, what
> alien and everchanging Lord
> sings me the anthems of the beasts and sovereign stones?

Her next volume was *The Fire Eaters* (1976) , containing both poetry and prose. The poems are exuberant and often personal. The myths are there, but the Toronto world of seminars, dentists, comic books and neighbourhood gangs comes through as well.

While her work is generally mythopoeic, it is not really similar to that of Jay Macpherson. Gwendolyn MacEwen is more likely to go back beyond Christian and classical myth to primitive fertility myths or to ancient Egypt and Babylon in her search for ways to handle the mysteries of life and death. She is interested in the occult, the magical and the mystical, rather than in the traditional myth which tried to explain physical phenomena. She writes her own arcana, poems delving into mysteries, highly visionary riddles for the twentieth-century rational reader.

The work of today's Canadian women poets is rich and diverse, and cannot be categorized. For some, like Dorothy Livesay and Phyllis Gotlieb, poetry is the celebration of life. Some poets reflect Canadian problems and social conscience, as does the recent work of Miriam Waddington. There is local poetry by such gifted observers as Elizabeth Brewster. Canada takes its place in an international or supranational setting with the mythic, universalized work of Jay Macpherson and Gwendolyn MacEwen. Older, traditional poetic forms have come to live side by side with the riotous growth of free forms. The joys and frustrations of urban living often replace those of the countryside.

1. How does Jay Macpherson use Christian allusions in *The Boatman*? How does she use classical Greek mythology? Is there any conflict between these two major sources in her work?

2. Compare Elizabeth Brewster's earlier rural poetry with her later urban poetry. Does her outlook change? Do her values change? Does her imagery change?

3. The mythopoeic way of looking at the physical world involves basic patterns. One classical pattern is that of the four elements. How are images of these four elements — earth, air, fire and water — used in Gwendolyn MacEwen's *The Fire-Eaters*?

4. Phyllis Gotlieb and Miriam Waddington are city people. How similar is their treatment of urban life? Are there significant differences in tone and imagery?

Trace the nursery rhymes, children's songs, Negro spirituals, and the poems from Blake's *Songs of Innocence*, in Phyllis Gotlieb's *Ordinary, Moving*. How has she used them? What effect do they have on poetry about Toronto streets?

Choose one of the women poets referred to in this chapter for a study of women's roles. What roles are available to women in general in her poetry? If she writes very subjectively, what roles are open to her? In what images and tone does she write on this subject?

For Reading

Brewster, Elizabeth. *Passage of Summer: Selected Poems.*
    Ryerson Press, 1969.
Brewster, Elizabeth. *In Search of Eros.* Clarke Irwin, 1974.
Brewster, Elizabeth. *Sometimes I Think of Moving.* Oberon,
    1977.
Gotlieb, Phyllis. *Ordinary, Moving.* Oxford University Press of
    Canada, 1969.
Gotlieb, Phyllis. *Why Should I Have All the Grief?* Macmillan
    of Canada, 1969.
MacEwen, Gwendolyn. *The Fire-Eaters.* Oberon, 1976.
MacEwen, Gwendolyn. *King of Egypt, King of Dreams.*
    Macmillan of Canada, 1971.
MacEwen, Gwendolyn. *Magic Animals: Selected Poems Old and
    New.* Macmillan of Canada, 1974.
Macpherson, J. Jay. *The Boatman and Other Poems.* Oxford
    University Press of Canada, 1968.
Macpherson, J. Jay. *Welcoming Disaster:Poems 1970-1974.*
    Toronto: Saanes Publications, 1975.

Atwood, Margaret. "MacEwen's Muse." *Canadian Literature,*
    no. 45 (Summer 1970) , 24-32.
Gibbs, Robert. "Next Time from a Different Country."
    Canadian Literature, no. 62 (Autumn 1974) , 17-32.
    (Elizabeth Brewster).
Gose, E. B. "They shall have arcana." *Canadian Literature,*
    no. 21 (Summer 1964) , 36-45. (Gwendolyn MacEwen) .
Jones, D. G. "Voices in the Dark." *Canadian Literature,* no. 45
    (Summer 1970) , 68-74. (Phyllis Gotlieb)
Reaney, James. "The Third Eye: Jay Macpherson's
    The Boatman." *Canadian Literature,* no. 3 (Winter 1960) ,
    23-34.
Warwick, Ellen D. "To Seek a Single Symmetry." *Canadian
    Literature,* no. 71 (Winter 1976) , 21-34. (Gwendolyn
    MacEwen)

Margaret Laurence

Few Canadian writers have an international standing or readership. Those who do are often those who have gone abroad to write and publish, following Morley Callaghan's successful example. Writers such as Mordecai Richler, Marie-Claire Blais and Margaret Laurence have spent a number of years in other countries. The usual choices are England, France and the United States. In the case of Margaret Laurence, Africa was her first foreign home.

She was born in Neepawa, Manitoba, in 1926, and raised there. She wanted to be a writer. Through a scholarship, she was able to go to Winnipeg and university, to study literature. In 1947, on graduation, she married Jack Laurence, a fellow student originally from Alberta. In 1949 they left for England to look for work. Jack took on a civil engineering job with the British Colonial Service, a project to build dams in Somaliland. They left England for Africa almost immediately.

Neepawa, Manitoba in the 1950s

They were in Somaliland from 1950 to 1952. Margaret Laurence worked on her fiction, at that time, mainly short stories. At the same time she was intrigued by the Somali people, who, in spite of bare subsistence living, had a lively oral literature. She learned the Somali language, and translated their poems and folk tales into English. Two years after she left Somaliland, the British officials to whom she had entrusted her work managed to get it printed in Nigeria. This first book, *A Tree for Poverty: Somali Poetry and Prose,* is her tribute to Somaliland and its oral tradition.

She returned to England in 1952 for the birth of her daughter, and then the Laurences went to Ghana for a five-year term, during which a son was born. The Somali translation appeared and her first African short story was accepted for publication in Canada. She continued to be fascinated by the contrast between Canadian and African cultures, and by the approaching end to British imperial control.

The Laurences returned to Canada in 1957, and lived in Vancouver until 1962. In 1960 *This Side Jordan,* a novel set in Ghana just before its independence, was published. It is not particularly sympathetic to the British who held power there for so long, and reaped the profits. However, in this novel, independence is not an easy process for either black or white. Nathaniel Amegbe, the main character, has his own cultural problems to work out regardless of the white man. He has rejected the strong call of his rural and tribal upbringing, and chosen the new life of the city and the education of the next generation.

In 1962 the Laurences returned to England. Margaret Laurence wanted to write; her husband was a project engineer whose career would always involve packing and moving. They agreed to separate, and she remained in London. London turned out to be interesting, but not the best place to work. Eventually she found a countryside home, and settled there to raise her children and write. For more than ten years, England was her home.

In 1963 her work on African experiences was published in two formats, fiction and non-fiction. *The Prophet's Camel Bell* (in the United States, *New Wind in a Dry Land*) is her personal account of the two years in Somaliland, based on a diary she had kept. *The Tomorrow-Tamer and Other Stories* contains ten of her African short stories and continues the emphases of *This Side Jordan.* Again there is the clash of white and black, not so much in political terms but in terms of cultural values, ways of thinking, and the hold of the past. Poignant and sometimes tragic, the stories record most pointedly the African dilemma of tribal values set against Western influences.

In England Margaret Laurence was becoming known as a writer on Africa. She was also deriving inspiration from her Canadian background, and the hold of her own Scottish and

Irish ancestral roots and upbringing. Neepawa becomes "Manawaka,"and the first of the Manawaka novels, *The Stone Angel*, appeared in 1964. It was published simultaneously in Canada, Britain, and the United States. On the same day, her American publisher brought out editions of her two previous African books. Margaret Laurence, author, had arrived.

The Stone Angel records the thoughts and memories of Hagar Shipley, ninety years old and the antithesis of the little-old-lady stereotype. Hagar is a strong, determined, overly proud character who has never made life easy for herself or for anyone around her. As the daughter of the town's leading merchant, she has had status; she has also developed an imperious spirit, which leads her into an unsuitable marriage in defiance of her father. As she is dying, she gains some understanding of herself:

> Pride was my wilderness, and the demon that led me there was fear. I was alone, never anything else, and never free, for I carried my chains within me, and they spread out from me and shackled all I touched.

Fear and pride together prevent Hagar from ever saying what she really feels. Lack of communication and an inability to express love dominate her life. She is awesome, a magnificent creation we can admire, but only with great difficulty love.

Margaret Laurence creates a contrasting personality in her second Manawaka novel, *A Jest of God* (1966; in the United States, *Rachel, Rachel*). Hagar was motherless; Rachel, though in her thirties, is still tied to an unbearable hypochondriac of a mother. She does not have a life of her own and lives vicariously through her work as a teacher. She wants a husband and children, but cannot reach out as a Hagar Shipley would.

Laurence with students during her year as Writer-in-Residence at the University of Toronto

A summer affair raises hopes but little more. The young man leaves, and a suspected pregnancy turns out to be a benign tumour. However, these experiences of life on her own give Rachel the courage to make her own way, and to leave stifling Manawaka. Over her mother's objections she makes arrangements for a teaching job in the big city, Vancouver.

> Where I'm going, anything may happen. Nothing may happen. Maybe I will marry a middle-aged widower, or a longshoreman, or a cattle-hoof-trimmer, or a barrister or a thief. And have my children in time. Or maybe not.

While Rachel will take her mother with her, their roles have been reversed. She is being liberated into life, although she is aware of the chance that this may be just another ironic jest.

Margaret Laurence's continuing interest in Africa led to a critical work, *Long Drums and Cannons: Nigerian Dramatists and Novelists* (1968). Canada and the ex-British African nations have shared the experience of being colonies, and then trying to work out of a post-colonialist mentality. In the nineteen fifties and sixties, there was a good deal of literature written by Africans in the English language (which through educational systems came to be the common language among many tribes). *Long Drums and Cannons* is a tribute to the Nigerian achievement in these years. It was published just before the Nigerian civil war.

Her next novel, *The Fire-Dwellers* (1969), is written from the point of view of Stacey, a character somewhere between proud Hagar and submissive Rachel in emotional makeup. Stacey has married, she has four children and lives in Vancouver, where her husband has a job he hates. Nothing could seem more ordinary. But Stacey finds the outside world threatening, if not insane. They are all in a hell, as the title suggests, where nobody relates or communicates.

Stacey's various escape attempts, including a brief love affair with a much younger man, are part of her efforts to cope with her situation. Yet her emotional ties with her uncommunicative husband and her children make her rebellions short-lived. Like Margaret Laurence's other heroines, she finally comes to grips with her life and her various roles.

> I'm going to quit worrying about it. I used to think there would be a blinding flash of light someday, and then I would be wise and calm and would know how to cope with everything and my kids would rise up and call me blessed. Now I see that whatever I'm like, I'm pretty well stuck with it for life. Hell of a revelation that turned out to be.

The Fire-Dwellers is enlivened by comic touches, especially when Stacey's spoken words are immediately followed by the interior monologue revealing what she really would like to say.

During the academic year 1969-70, Margaret Laurence was back in Canada as writer-in-residence at the University of Toronto. In 1970 she bought a summer cottage near Peterborough, and began an international commuting schedule of

Every novelist has this terrible feeling from time to time: Who am I? because you feel almost that you may exist only in your characters and not have a character of your own. You fly to the mirror to see if you're still there. And this is really spooky.

Margaret Laurence, in Donald Cameron, Conversations With Canadian Novelists *(Macmillan of Canada, 1973)*

summers in Canada and winters in England. In 1970 two more books were published. *A Bird in the House* is the fourth of the Manawaka series; *Jason's Quest* is a book for children. In *Jason's Quest* the city of Molanium is threatened — by boredom. Even the moles get bored, and have to be rescued from their excessive reverence for past tradition.

A Bird in the House is a series of eight stories about the childhood and adolescence of Vanessa MacLeod. While this is the only work by Margaret Laurence that is autobiographical in nature, her early life has been substantially re-shaped in the stories. The central character, Vanessa, equally sensitive and strong-minded, is a trapped bird seeking freedom. The overpowering force to fear, hate, and rebel against is her Grandfather Connor, a stern cantankerous patriarch. His house is much as he is:

> Known to the rest of the town as "the old Connor place" and to the family as the Brick House, it was plain as the winter turnips in its root cellar, sparsely windowed as some crusader's embattled fortress in a heathen wilderness, its rooms in a perpetual gloom except in the brief height of summer.

Years later when Vanessa revisits the town, she does not seek her grandfather's memorial in the graveyard but rather in the Brick House, his symbol and her old prison .

After many years of living abroad, Margaret Laurence decided to return to Canada for good. During the previous twenty-three years, she had spent only five in her own country. In 1973 she moved to Lakefield, close to her summer cottage in the Peterborough district. The summer shack, nicknamed "Manawaka," remains her summer writing refuge. It also provides one of the settings for her final Manawaka novel, *The Diviners* (1974) .

The Diviners is in part a novel of the outcast in Manawaka society. Hagar, Rachel, Stacey and Vanessa had all come from the right side of the tracks. Morag Gunn of *The Diviners* looks back on her life, which starts unpromisingly enough as an orphan raised by the garbage collector. She escapes and raises her status by marrying an English professor and moving to Toronto. Ironically, this kind of life turns out to be an imprisonment of a new kind.

The other poor and dispossessed in Manawaka are the Métis, represented by the Tonnerre family. Morag goes back to her roots in one sense and has a daughter by Jules Tonnerre, an old friend who sings folksongs about Louis Riel. She devotes her life to her daughter and her writing. She also goes back to her roots in choosing to live in a rural setting.

> *Maybe I should've brought Pique up entirely in cities, where she'd have known how bad things are all over, where she'd have learned young about survival, about the survival tactics in a world now largely dedicated to Death, Slavery and the Pursuit of Unhappiness. Instead, I've made an island. Are islands real?*

Throughout *The Diviners* Morag meditates on what she is, what her various experiences have made her into. She has been lucky

Margaret Laurence, D. Litt.
University of Toronto

to find her special talent, writing novels — analogous to the mysterious gift that "the diviners" have for finding water.

Margaret Laurence has said that *The Diviners* is the last of the Manawaka world. In 1976 she went back over a number of her personal and historical essays and travel pieces, and put together *Heart of a Stranger*. It shows as usual the perception and sensitivity of a traveller open to other cultures. But it is her fiction, her novels and her short stories, that has made her famous.

There is a consistency in her work, the African and the Canadian, in her efforts to express both the possibilities and the limitations of the individual, the need for freedom set against the need for roots. In her own words,

> Individuals can to a considerable extent liberate themselves.
> But I don't think that they can ever wholly get away from some
> of the things they have inherited, cultural things, concepts and
> so on. And I don't think that real liberation comes from turning
> your back on your whole past or on your ancestral past.

She sees both men and women as trapped souls in need of liberation, and her characters survive the long march to freedom.

For Discussion

1. Rachel in *A Jest of God* and Stacey in *The Fire-Dwellers* are sisters, raised in the Cameron household in Manawaka. How do you account for their becoming such different characters by the time they are in their thirties?

2. Childhood and adolescent experiences are important in Margaret Laurence's Manawaka books. In what similar ways do these experiences affect Hagar in *The Stone Angel* and Vanessa in *A Bird in the House*? What significant differences are there, and why do you consider these differences to be significant?

3. What does the word "independence" mean to the various Ghanaians in *This Side Jordan* and *The Tomorrow-Tamer and Other Stories?* What does "independence" mean to you?

4. Both Morag Gunn in *The Diviners* and Maggie Vardoe in Ethel Wilson's *Swamp Angel* leave their husbands and urban life. They choose to live in an isolated rural setting. Yet they seem to be very different characters, with different goals, satisfactions, and roles. Just how different are they? Why does *The Diviners*, written only twenty years after *Swamp Angel*, seem much more contemporary?

For Research

Survey five to ten women whom you know to be wives and mothers. How do they see themselves in these roles? What are their major satisfactions as wives and as mothers? What are their major dissatisfactions? Compare your findings with the opinions offered by Stacey in *The Fire-Dwellers* and Minn in Marian Engel's *The Honeyman Festival*. On the basis of your comparison, are Stacey and Minn representative wives and mothers? If not, in what ways are they unusual?

Debate:
Resolved that living abroad gives Canadian writers a better perspective on Canada. (Take into consideration the work of Margaret Laurence, Marie-Claire Blais, and Marian Engel.)

Laurence, Margaret. *A Bird in the House.* New Canadian Library #96. McClelland & Stewart, 1974.

Laurence, Margaret. *The Diviners.* McClelland & Stewart, 1974. Also in paperback: Bantam, 1975.

Laurence, Margaret. *The Fire-Dwellers.* New Canadian Library #87. McClelland & Stewart, 1973.

Laurence, Margaret. *A Jest of God.* New Canadian Library #111. McClelland & Stewart, 1974.

Laurence, Margaret. *The Stone Angel.* New Canadian Library #59. McClelland & Stewart, 1968.

Laurence, Margaret. *This Side Jordan.* New Canadian Library #126. McClelland & Stewart, 1976.

Laurence, Margaret. *The Tomorrow-Tamer and Other Stories.* New Canadian Library #70. McClelland & Stewart, 1970.

Laurence, Margaret. "Where the World Began." *Maclean's Magazine,* vol. 85 (December 1972), 22-23, 80.

Gom, Leona M. "Laurence and the Use of Memory." *Canadian Literature,* no. 71 (Winter 1976), 21-34.

Gotlieb, Phyllis. "On Margaret Laurence." *Tamarack Review,* vol. 52 (iii, 1969), 76-80.

Kreisel, Henry. "The African Stories of Margaret Laurence."

Hind-Smith, Joan. *Three Voices: The Lives of Margaret. Canadian Forum,* vol. 41 (April 1961), 8-10. *Laurence, Gabrielle Roy, Frederick Philip Grove.* Clarke Irwin, 1975.

Read, S. E. "The Maze of Life: The Work of Margaret Laurence." *Canadian Literature,* no. 27 (Winter 1966), 5-14.

Thomas, Clara. *The Manawaka World of Margaret Laurence.* McClelland & Stewart, 1975. Also in paperback: New Canadian Library #131.

Thomas, Clara. *Margaret Laurence.* New Canadian Library #W3. McClelland & Stewart, 1969.

Woodcock, George. "Jungle and Prairie." *Canadian Literature,* no. 45 (Summer 1970), 82-84.

Chapter 9

Margaret Atwood

Margaret Atwood is another internationally known Canadian woman writer. Through poems, novels and critical articles she has probably reached more readers than any other current Canadian writer.

Born in Ottawa in 1939, Margaret Atwood went to the University of Toronto, and then to Radcliffe and Harvard in the United States. Her first career was that of the scholar and English professor, at Sir George Williams University, the Universities of British Columbia and Alberta, and York University. She married at the age of twenty-seven. At the same time, she was writing both poetry and prose.

The first to be published were poems, in *The Circle Game* (1966) and *The Animals in That Country* (1968). *The Circle Game,* which won the Governor General's award in 1967 introduces some favourite image patterns. Nature images, animals, water, and forest, are used sympathetically while city images are not. Imagery is frequently used to describe inner mental and emotional states, as in "Journey to the Interior." *The Animals in That Country* is in much the same vein, with an added emphasis on both real and imaginary animals. The wilderness even contains "animals" such as trappers. In "Progressive Insanities of a Pioneer," Margaret Atwood begins her use of a recurring theme, escape through madness.

In 1969 her first novel, *The Edible Woman,* appeared. It is as much a satire on the consumer-oriented urban life as it is a serio-comic novel about young adulthood. Its main character, Marian McAlpin, is an average young woman. She works in market research, and has an upwardly mobile boy friend. Marriage and other options are presented. Marian's unconscious revulsion from all this causes her to gradually lose the ability to eat. At a dinner party,

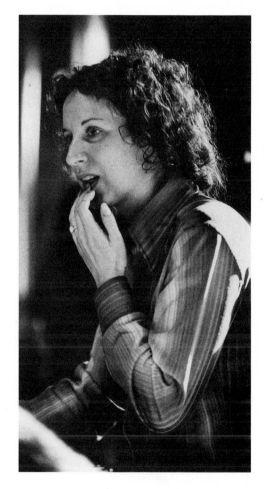

> Marian surveyed the chunks of meat on her plate with growing desperation. She thought of sliding them under the tablecloth — but they would be discovered. She would have been able to put them into her purse if only she hadn't left it over by the chair. Perhaps she could slip them down the front of her blouse or up her sleeves . . .

She makes her escape through a tenuous but sincere friendship with an eccentric graduate student. At the end she can stand on her own two feet — and eat.

The Journals of Susanna Moodie (1970) is Margaret Atwood's first book of poems designed as a single unit, with one voice. The narrator is a re-creation of the nineteenth-century pioneer and writer. There are three journals, and the third with its "Thoughts from Underground" is the most original. It takes Susanna Moodie far beyond *Roughing It in the Bush* and *Life in the Clearings* to old age, death and beyond.

Procedures for Underground, also published in 1970, has some poems set in Edmonton, Boston and Toronto. More are set in gardens, parks, forests and beaches. The dominant image is that of change, from man to bird or animal or monster. We are reminded that man is just the last metamorphosis of life over a million years. Extinct animals are

> . . . passed on
> in us, part of us now
> part of the structure of the bones
>
> existing still in us
> as fossil skulls . . .

The volume ends with an unusually hopeful vision of a perfect dance.

Power Politics (1971) is Margaret Atwood's second book of poems in one voice. The narrator is female, and the situation involves a relationship between herself and a man. Both are involved in "power politics," in gamesmanship, in scoring emotional points. Images of evasion, hostility and imprisonment evoke the unhealthiness of the relationship. In this "love affair" neither love nor sex offers joy. *Power Politics* gives an uncompromising view of some of the psychological needs that can hold people together, for worse rather than for better.

1972 saw the culmination of a number of Margaret Atwood's major themes in the publication of two different kinds of prose. *Surfacing* is the novel, and *Survival: A Thematic Guide to Canadian Literature* is the deliberately non-academic treatment of some important themes in our literature.

Survival is written around the thesis that Canadian literature is at heart about oppressor/victim relationships. Since most of us are victims, we have to be concerned with basic survival, and the obstacles to it.

In earlier writers these obstacles are external — the land, the climate, and so forth. In later writers the obstacles tend to become both harder to identify and more internal; they are no longer obstacles to physical survival but obstacles to what we may call spiritual survival, to life as anything more than a minimally human being.

Canada is presented as a victim of its own sense of inferiority to England and France, and more recently in political and economic terms as a victim of the United States. This black and provocative survey brought more fame to Margaret Atwood, and provoked controversy over its accuracy, profundity and bias.

The novel *Surfacing* also revolves around the themes of oppressor/victim and survival. The unnamed narrator is a young woman looking for her father, who has disappeared in the bush of northern Quebec. She tends to be a victim, of her own self-deceptions as well as of other people. An anti-American element emerges: Americans exploit the country. Gradually we find out that the "Americans" in the novel are from southern Ontario, and that "American" means any soulless materialistic despoiler.

The narrator of *Surfacing* gradually withdraws from her companions and goes back to the wilderness she has known and loved as a child. She dives into the waters of the lake, looking for signs left by her father or by Indians. In the last section she "dives" into madness, and surfaces with new understanding.

> This above all, to refuse to be a victim. Unless I can do that I can do nothing. I have to recant, give up the old belief that I am powerless and because of it nothing I can do will ever hurt anyone. A lie which was always more disastrous than the truth would have been. The word games, the winning and losing games are finished . . .

The ending indicates her return to civilization, reborn in the womb of nature.

Margaret Atwood was at this time in 1972 working as a director for the nationalistic House of Anansi press in Toronto, and lecturing on the state of Canadian literature. She was writer-in-residence at the University of Toronto. Her formal career as scholar and teacher was left behind; she was becoming a very important poet-novelist-critic and Canadian personality. She separated from her husband, and they were later divorced.

You Are Happy (1974) was her first book of poetry in three years. There are still poems that analyze difficult human relationships, but there is the possibility of new beginnings and happiness. One section, "Songs of the Transformed," is written from the point of view of animals. Predictably, human nature is somewhat acidly presented. The fox is willing to treat man as a god, but

> you wore gloves and plodded,
> you saw me as vermin,
> a crook in a fur visor;
> the fate you aim at me
> is not light literature.

"Canadian" is a very ambiguous word. If people think I'm supposed to embody something like beavers, or the RCMP, well. . . . I mean I'd hate to end up being any kind of national symbol or, God forbid, a monument. I don't think that's what writing is for at all.

Margaret Atwood, in Maclean's, *September 6, 1976*

"Circe/Mud Poems," another sequence, reworks the Circe and Ulysses myth from Circe's point of view. The final series in *You Are Happy* takes a look at the human body. Flesh is mortal and vulnerable (as minds are), but it is accepted in images of life and wholeness.

In 1974, in her role as public personality, Margaret Atwood cancelled her official trip to the Soviet Union over its expulsion of the dissident writer Alexander Solzhenitsyn. Never a lover of city life, she moved to the countryside north of Toronto. She has retired from political platforms. She lives with the novelist Graeme Gibson, and in 1976 gave birth to their daughter.

In *Lady Oracle* (1976), her third novel, she returned to the more comic view of life first evident in *The Edible Woman*. Joan Foster, alias Louisa Delacourt, tells her story by starting with her recently faked suicide. Her problem in her narration is that she has too many stories. She is a writer of "Costume Gothic" romances, a bestselling poet, a media personality, and the wife of a left-wing intellectual, while hiding an affair with a would-be artist. Her various "lives" have been catching up with each other, and she has chosen to exit dramatically.

Unfortunately she handles plots in real life with a lot less verve and control than the near-rape and near-murder plots of her romances. Friends are charged with her murder, and she has to go back to Canada to sort out the terrible mess she has made. Throughout the novel, Margaret Atwood pokes fun at the Canadian publishing scene, the reviewers, the media people, the left-wing action groups, and the present state of the arts.

In 1976 poems from each of the previous volumes, were re-issued in her *Selected Poems*. About half of her work to date is included. It has all of *The Journals of Susanna Moodie,* and two complete sequences from *You Are Happy*, the "Songs of the Transformed" and the "Circe/Mud Poems."

Margaret Atwood is working on several books and what she calls a "masque," a co-operative effort to create something like a ballet with poetry and music. She continues to write about Canadian literature for magazines and scholarly journals. She has worked on the script for a Canadian film production of Margaret Laurence's *The Diviners*. Her early reputation for tough-minded poetry has become international. Her novels are being re-published in the United States.

One of the reasons for her large Canadian following is the fact that she epitomizes so many of the issues in Canadian society and literature. She is concerned with protection of the environment, with national identity, and with the increasing insanity of urban life. She is concerned, as an individual, with the woman's point of view. The women's liberation movement has not been a factor in her writing such books as *Power Politics* and *Surfacing*, but it may have been a factor in their reception.

Margaret Atwood writes about what it is to be Canadian, in
both comic and tragic ways. She ends *Survival* with two questions
for all Canadians:

Have we survived?
If so, what happens *after* survival?

Atwood lecturing during her year as
Writer-in-Residence at the
University of Toronto

For Discussion

1. Examine Margaret Atwood's *The Journals of Susanna Moodie* in the light of Susanna Moodie's *Roughing It in the Bush* and *Life in the Clearings*. What has Margaret Atwood chosen to emphasize? What has she ignored? What has she added? Based on your findings, what, in your opinion, is the poet's overall intention?

2. Trace the evolution of the theme of survival through the *Selected Poems,* in chronological order. In how many ways does the individual have to survive? What are the roads to survival? Trace the evolution of the survival theme through *The Edible Woman, Surfacing,* and *Lady Oracle.* Are there new variations of this theme in the novels?

3. Trace the evolution of the theme of madness in "Progressive Insanities of a Pioneer", the third section of *The Journals of Susanna Moodie,* and *Surfacing.* What are the causes of madness? What are the results? Are there circumstances under which madness can be seen as healthy?

4. Compare Margaret Atwood's treatment of the wilderness in *Surfacing* with that of Marian Engel in *Bear.*

5. Male-female relationships, seen from the woman's point of view, are the focus of Margaret Atwood's *Power Politics* and Dorothy Livesay's *The Unquiet Bed.* In what ways are these two volumes of poetry similar? In what ways are they quite different?

For Research

In recent times it has become possible for a talented Canadian woman writer to earn a living by writing. Margaret Atwood, Margaret Laurence, and Marie-Claire Blais, for instance, are now in this position. Investigate the social, cultural, and economic factors which have made this possible. Which factor do you consider to be the most significant? Why?

One of Margaret Atwood's interests is the promotion of Canadian literature. Visit your nearest bookstore. What percentage of books are Canadian? Within the Canadian section, how much is devoted to literature (novels, short stories, poetry, drama, and anthologies) ? How much of this literature is by women authors? According to your findings, how would you assess the stature of Canadian women authors today? How does your bookseller rate them in terms of sales?

Atwood ,Margaret. *The Edible Woman*. New Canadian Library #93. McClelland & Stewart, 1973.

Atwood, Margaret. *Lady Oracle*. McClelland & Stewart, 1976.

Atwood, Margaret. "Oratorio for Sasquatch, Man, and Two Androids." In *Poems for Voices*. CBC, Toronto, 1970.

Atwood, Margaret. *Selected Poems*. Oxford University Press of Canada, 1976.

Atwood, Margaret. *Surfacing*. McClelland & Stewart, 1972. Also in paperback: Paperjacks. General Publishing, 1973.

Atwood, Margaret. *Survival: A Thematic Guide to Canadian Literature*. Anansi, 1972.

Ayre, John. "Margaret Atwood and the End of Colonialism." *Saturday Night,* vol. 87 (November 1972) , 23-26.

Grosskurth, Phyllis. "Victimization or Survival." *Canadian Literature,* no. 55 (Winter 1973) , 108-110.

MacGregor, Roy. "Mother Oracle: Margaret Atwood is telling us about ourselves — rather than about herself." *The Canadian,* September 25, 1976, 15-18.

The Malahat Review (University of Victoria) , no. 41 (January 1977) . Special issue on Margaret Atwood.

Miner, Valerie. "The Many Facets of Margaret Atwood." *Chatelaine,* vol. 48 (June 1975) , 32-33, 66, 68-69.

Onley, Gloria. "Power Politics in Bluebeard's Castle." *Canadian Literature,* no. 60 (Summer 1974) , 21-42.

Purdy, A. W. "Atwood's Moodie." *Canadian Literature,* no. 47 (Winter 1971) , 80-84.

Ross, Gary. "The Circle Game." *Canadian Literature,* no. 60 (Summer 1974) , 51-63.

Ross, Gary. "The Divided Self." *Canadian Literature,* no. 71 (Winter 1976) , 39-47.

For Reading

THE
Canadian Settler's Guide:

BY

MRS. C. P. TRAILL,

AUTHORESS OF

THE "BACKWOODS OF CANADA," &c., &c., &c.

FIFTH EDITION.

CHRISTMAS DAY IN THE BACKWOODS.

TORONTO, C.W.:

PRINTED AT THE OLD COUNTRYMAN OFFICE.

1855.

Cameron, Donald. *Conversations with Canadian Novelists*. Macmillan of Canada, 1973. (Margaret Laurence, Gabrielle Roy).

Frye, Northrop. *The Bush Garden: Essays on the Canadian Imagination*. Anansi, 1971.

Gibson, Graeme (interviewer). *Eleven Canadian Novelists*. Anansi, 1973. (Margaret Atwood, Marian Engel, Margaret Laurence, Alice Munro).

Gnarowski, Michael. *A Concise Bibliography of English-Canadian Literature*. McClelland & Stewart, 1973.

Gwyn, Sandra. *Women in the Arts in Canada*. Monograph for the Royal Commission on the Status of Women. Ottawa: Information Canada, 1971.

Hind-Smith, Joan. *Three Voices: The Lives of Margaret Laurence, Gabrielle Roy, Frederick Philip Grove*. Clarke Irwin, 1975.

Innis, Mary Quayle, ed. *The Clear Spirit: Twenty Canadian Women and Their Times*. University of Toronto Press, 1966. (Susanna Moodie, Catherine Parr Traill, Pauline Johnson, Nellie McClung, L. M. Montgomery, Mazo de la Roche, Emily Carr).

Klinck, C. F., ed. *Literary History of Canada: Canadian Literature in English*. 2nd ed. 3v. University of Toronto Press, 1976.

League of Canadian Poets. *Catalogue of Members*. 1976.

McCourt, E. A. *The Canadian West in Fiction*. Rev. ed. Ryerson Press, 1970. (Nellie McClung, Martha Ostenso, Laura Goodman Salverson, Gabrielle Roy, Adele Wiseman, Margaret Laurence).

Moss, John. *Patterns of Isolation in English Canadian Fiction*. McClelland & Stewart, 1974.

New, William. *Articulating West: Essays on Purpose and Form in Modern Canadian Literature*. New Press, 1972. (Ethel Wilson, Margaret Avison, Margaret Laurence).

Pacey, Desmond. *Essays in Canadian Criticism 1938-1968*. Ryerson Press, 1969. (Marjorie Pickthall, Ethel Wilson, Dorothy Livesay).

Ricou, Laurence. *Vertical Man / Horizontal World: Man and Landscape in Canadian Prairie Fiction*. University of British Columbia Press, 1973. (Martha Ostenso, Gabrielle Roy, Adele Wiseman, Margaret Laurence).

Smith, A. J. M. *Towards a View of Canadian Letters: Selected Critical Essays 1928-1971*. University of British Columbia Press, 1973. (P. K. Page, Margaret Avison).

Stephens, Donald G. *Writers of the Prairies*. Canadian Literature Series. University of British Columbia Press, 1973. (Martha Ostenso, Gabrielle Roy, Adele Wiseman, Margaret Laurence).

Story, Norah. *The Oxford Companion to Canadian History and Literature*. Oxford University Press of Canada, 1967.

Sylvestre, G., B. Conron & C. F. Klinck. *Canadian Writers/ Ecrivains Canadiens*. Rev. ed. Ryerson Press, 1966.

Watters, R. E. *A Checklist of Canadian Literature and Background Materials 1628-1960*. Rev. ed. University of Toronto Press, 1972.

Watters, R. E., & I. F. Bell. *On Canadian Literature 1806-1960: A Checklist of Articles, Books and Theses on English-Canadian Literature, Its Authors, and Language*. University of Toronto Press, 1966.

Wilson, Edmund. *O Canada: An American's Notes on Canadian Culture*. New York: Farrar, Straus & Giroux, 1965. (Marie-Claire Blais, Anne Hébert).

Woodcock, George, ed. *The Canadian Novel in the Twentieth Century*. New Canadian Library #115. McClelland & Stewart, 1975. (Mazo de la Roche, Ethel Wilson, Sheila Watson, Gwendolyn MacEwen, Margaret Laurence, Margaret Atwood).

Woodcock, George, ed. *A Choice of Critics: Selections from Canadian Literature*. Oxford University Press of Canada, 1966. (Jay Macpherson, Margaret Avison, Gabrielle Roy).

Woodcock, George, ed. *Poets and Critics: Essays from Canadian Literature 1966-1974*. Oxford University Press of Canada, 1974. (P. K. Page, Margaret Avison, Dorothy Livesay, Gwendolyn MacEwen, Margaret Atwood).

Woodcock, George, ed. *The Sixties: Writers and Writing of the Decade*. University of British Columbia Press, 1969. (Margaret Laurence, P. K. Page, Dorothy Livesay, Miriam Waddington).

French, William. "The Women in Our Literary Life." *The Imperial Oil Review,* vol. 59 (no. 1, 1975) , 2-7. Also in *The Canadian Author and Bookman,* vol. 51 (Spring, 1976) , 1-3, 5-6.

Jones, D. G. "Myth, Frye, and Canadian Writers." *Canadian Literature,* no. 55 (Winter 1973), 7-22. (Gabrielle Roy, Anne Hébert, Gwendolyn MacEwen) .

Jones, D. G. "The Sleeping Giant: Or the Uncreated Conscience of the Race." *Canadian Literature,* no. 26 (Autumn 1965) , 3-21. (Margaret Avison, Jay Macpherson, P. K. Page, Phyllis Webb, Gabrielle Roy, Gwendolyn MacEwen) .

Mackenzie, Ruth. "Life in a New Land: Notes on the Immigrant Theme in Canadian Fiction." *Canadian Literature,* no. 7 (Winter 1961) , 24-33.

McKenna, Isobel. "Women in Canadian Literature." *Canadian Literature,* no. 62 (Autumn 1974) , 69-78.

Mitcham, Allison. "Northern Utopia." *Canadian Literature,* no. 63 (Winter 1975) , 35-39. (Gabrielle Roy, Margaret Atwood) .

Modern Fiction Studies (Purdue University) . Special Issue: Modern Canadian Fiction. Vol. 22 (Autumn 1976) . (Alice Munro, Margaret Laurence, Margaret Atwood, Gabrielle Roy, Marie-Claire Blais).

Shain, Merle. "Some of Our Best Poets Are . . . Women." *Chatelaine,* vol. 45 (October 1972) , 48-9, 103-7.

Stevens, Peter. "Canadian Artists as Writers." *Canadian Literature,* no. 46 (Autumn 1970) , 19-34. (Emily Carr, P. K. Page) .

Thomas, Clara. "Happily Ever After: Canadian Women in Fiction and Fact." *Canadian Literature,* no. 34 (Autumn 1967) , 43-53.

Records

Canadian Poets I. CBC, 1966. (Phyllis Webb, Gwendolyn MacEwen) .

The Journals of Susanna Moodie. Canadian Poets II. CBC, 1969. (Mia Anderson reading Margaret Atwood) .

Open Secret. CBC, 1972. (Gwendolyn MacEwen)

Six Toronto Poets. Folkways, 1958. (Anne Wilkinson, Margaret Avison, Jay Macpherson) .

Tapes

Canadian Writers on Tape Series. Ontario Institute for Studies in Education (c/o Van Nostrand Reinhold, Scarborough, Ont.)

Margaret Laurence
Dorothy Livesay
Gwendolyn MacEwen
Miriam Waddington

Margaret Atwood: Twist of Feeling. CBC, 1971.

My Country 'Tis of Thee. CBC, 1971. (Miriam Waddington).

Videotapes

Speaking of Books: Margaret Atwood (30 min. colour) BPN 125409, Ontario Educational Communications Authority (OECA)

Speaking of Books: Sylvia Fraser (30 min. colour) BPN 125412, Ontario Educational Communications Authority (OECA)

Speaking of Books: Gwendolyn MacEwen (30 min. colour) BPN 125410, Ontario Educational Communications Authority (OECA)

Insight: Joan Finnegan Mackenzie (30 min. colour) BPN 008276, Ontario Educational Communications Authority (OECA)

Films

The Journals of Susanna Moodie: Poems by Margaret Atwood. 15 min. B/W) Universal Education and Visual Arts (UEVA)

Kamouraska, directed by Claude Jutra. Canada, 1972. (based on and scripted by Anne Hébert, *Kamouraska*) .

Klee Wyck: The Story of Emily Carr. (16 min. colour) National Film Board of Canada.

Rachel, Rachel, directed by Paul Newman. U.S.A., 1968. (based on Margaret Laurence's *A Jest of God*) .

Acknowledgements

The author extends her thanks to the staff of the Massey Library, Royal Military College of Canada; Special Collections, Douglas Library, Queen's University; the Kingston Public Library; and the Resource Centre, St. Lawrence College of Applied Arts and Technology.

Excerpts used in the text were quoted from the following sources:

Chapter 1

p.1: Frances Brooke. *The History of Emily Montague.* NCL #27, McClelland & Stewart, 1961. p. 19.

p. 9: Catherine Parr Traill. *The Backwoods of Canada.* NCL #51, McClelland & Stewart, 1966. p. 98.

p. 11: Susanna Moodie. From her "Introduction" to her novel *Mark Hurdlestone,* reprinted at the end of her *Life in the Clearings.* Ed. R.L. McDougall, Macmillan, 1959. pp. 286-287.

p. 12: Susanna Moodie. *Roughing It in the Bush.* NCL #31. McClelland & Stewart, 1962. p. 237.

p. 13: Anna Jameson. *Winter Studies and Summer Rambles in Canada: Selections.* NCL #46. McClelland & Stewart, 1965. pp. 134-5.

Chapter 2

p. 17: *The Collected Poems of Isabella Valancy Crawford.* 1905. Reprinted. University of Toronto Press, 1972. p. 193.

p. 20: Sara Jeannette Duncan. *The Imperialist.* NCL #20. McClelland & Stewart, 1961. p. 176.

p. 21: *The Complete Poems of Marjorie Pickthall.* Ed. A. Pickthall. McClelland & Stewart, 1927. p. 13.

p. 23: L.M. Montgomery. *Anne of Green Gables.* Ryerson Press, 1942. p. 243.

p. 24: Nellie McClung. *Clearing in the West: My Own Story.* Allen, 1935. pp. 150-151.

Chapter 3

p. 29: R. Hambleton. *Mazo de la Roche of Jalna.* General Publishing, 1966. p. 172.

p. 31: Emily Carr. *Hundreds and Thousands: The Journals of Emily Carr.* Clarke, Irwin, 1966. p. 260.

p. 31: Martha Ostenso. *Wild Geese,* NCL #18. McClelland & Stewart, 1961. p. 12.

p. 32: Laura Goodman Salverson. *The Dark Weaver.* Ryerson, 1937. p. 64.

p. 33: Laura Goodman Salverson. *Confessions of an Immigrant's Daughter.* Ryerson, 1939. p. 119.

Chapter 4

p. 36: Dorothy Livesay. *The Collected Poems: The Two Seasons.* Ryerson, 1972.

p. 38: Dorothy Livesay. *The Unquiet Bed.* Ryerson, 1967. p. 36.

p. 39: G.L. Parker, ed. *The Evolution of Canadian Literature in English 1914-1945.* Holt, Rinehart & Winston, 1973. p. 320.

p. 40: P.K. Page. *Cry Ararat! Poems New and Selected.* McClelland & Stewart, 1967. p. 71.

p. 40: P.K. Page. *Cry Ararat! Poems New and Selected.* McClelland & Stewart, 1967. p. 21.

p. 41: Miriam Waddington. *Say Yes.* Oxford UP, 1969. p. 10.

p. 42: Margaret Avison. *The Dumbfounding.* Norton, 1966. p. 11.

p. 43: F.R. Scott. "The Canadian Authors Meet". *The Blasted Pine.* Macmillan, 1957.

Chapter 5

p. 48: Gabrielle Roy. *The Cashier.* NCL #40. McClelland & Stewart, 1963. pp. 40-41.

p. 49: Alan Brown, trans. *Poems by Anne Hébert.* Musson, 1975. p. 31.

p. 49: Anne Hébert. *Kamouraska.* Bantam, 1976. p. 3.

p. 50: Marie-Claire Blais. *Tête Blanche.* NCL #104. McClelland & Stewart, 1974. p. 132.

p. 51: Marie-Claire Blais. *A Season in the Life of Emmanuel.* Bantam, 1976. p. 1.

p. 52: Marie-Claire Blais. *St. Lawrence Blues.* Farrar, Straus & Giroux, 1974. p. 156.

Chapter 6

p. 56: Ethel Wilson. *Swamp Angel.* Macmillan, 1954. p. 204.

p. 57: Sheila Watson. *The Double Hook.* NCL #54. McClelland & Stewart, 1966. p. 113.

p. 58: Adele Wiseman. *The Sacrifice.* Viking, 1956. p. 292.

p. 59: Alice Munro. *Lives of Girls and Women.* McGraw-Hill Ryerson, 1971. p. 253.

p. 60: Marian Engel. *The Honeyman Festival.* Anansi, 1970. p 27.

p. 60: Marian Engel. *Monodromos.* Anansi, 1973. p. 237.

Chapter 7

p. 64: Elizabeth Brewster. *Passage of Summer: Selected Poems.* Ryerson, 1969. p. 29.

p. 65: Phyllis Gotlieb, *Ordinary, Moving.* Oxford UP, 1969. p. 69.

p. 66: Phyllis Gotlieb. *Why Should I Have All the Grief?* Macmillan, 1969. p. 3.

p. 67: Jay Macpherson. *The Boatman.* Oxford UP, 1957. p. 70.

p. 68: Gwendolyn MacEwen. *Magic Animals: Selected Poems Old and New.* Macmillan, 1974. p. 17.

p. 69: Gwendolyn MacEwen. *A Breakfast for Barbarians.* Ryerson, 1966. Before p. 1.

p. 70: Gwendolyn MacEwen. *Magic Animals: Selected Poems Old and New.* Macmillan, 1974. p. 136.

Chapter 8

p. 76: Margaret Laurence. *The Stone Angel.* McClelland & Stewart, 1968. p. 129.

p. 77: Margaret Laurence. *A Jest of God.* NCL #87. McClelland & Stewart, 1973. pp. 298-299.

p. 78: Margaret Laurence. *A Bird in the House.* NCL #96. McClelland & Stewart. p. 3.

p. 79: Margaret Laurence. *The Diviners.* Bantam, 1975. p. 356.

p. 80: Graeme Gibson. *Eleven Canadian Novelists.* Anansi, 1973. p. 203.

Chapter 9

p. 83: Margaret Atwood. *The Edible Woman.* McClelland & Stewart, 1973. p. 199.

p. 83: Margaret Atwood. *Procedures for Underground.* Oxford UP, 1970. p. 72.

p. 85: Margaret Atwood. *Survival: A Thematic Guide to Canadian Literature.* Anansi, 1972. p. 33.

p. 85: Margaret Atwood. *Surfacing.* McClelland & Stewart, 1972. p. 191.

p. 85: Margaret Atwood. *You Are Happy.* Oxford UP, 1974. p. 40

p. 87: Margaret Atwood. *Survival: A Thematic Guide to Canadian Literature.* Anansi, 1972. p. 246.

Index